RELOAD

Rethinking Violence in American Life

CHRISTOPHER B. STRAIN

Vanderbilt University Press ■ Nashville

© 2010 by Vanderbilt University Press
Nashville, Tennessee 37235
All rights reserved
First printing 2010

This book is printed on acid-free paper made
from 30% post-consumer recycled content.
Manufactured in the United States of America

Library of Congress Cataloging-in-Publication Data

Strain, Christopher B., 1970–
Reload : rethinking violence in American life /
Christopher B. Strain.
p. cm.
Includes bibliographical references and index.
ISBN 978-0-8265-1741-8 (cloth edition : alk. paper)
ISBN 978-0-8265-1742-5 (pbk. edition : alk. paper)
1. Violence—United States.
2. Violence in men—United States.
3. Violence in popular culture—United States.
I. Title.
HN90.V5S87 2010
306.0973—dc22
2010020351

To Lily

Contents

Preface

In the fall of 2008, as I worked on the manuscript for this book, someone blew up my father's office building. At first it was unclear what had happened. News outlets simply reported that there had been an explosion at a law firm in Dalton, Georgia. My dad, who was OK, relayed the information in a quick phone call. There were injuries. Jim Phillips, my father's cousin and law partner, had been badly hurt; he was being medevacked to the Joseph M. Still Burn Center in Augusta. Another person had been killed.

We pieced together the facts over the next few hours. On October 17, at approximately 10:00 a.m., a man named Lloyd Cantrell drove his SUV into the parking lot of the firm and rammed his vehicle into the side of the building. Cantrell was in a legal dispute over a piece of property with his son, Bruce, who was being represented by the firm. Folks around town knew he was eccentric, but the son apparently knew better than most the extent of his father's volatility. The two had grown estranged as Lloyd became less stable, threatening his son even as he threatened to harm himself. The younger Cantrell filed a lawsuit to keep his father off the property he had been given, after his father kicked down a door, stole tools, and brandished a gun. Bitter and despondent, Lloyd Cantrell had apparently decided that the law firm was to blame for his problems.

Backing up and speeding forward, Cantrell repeatedly rammed the building. Witnesses said that when his attempts to drive his SUV into the building failed, Cantrell got out of the vehicle. As Jim Phillips implored Cantrell to stop whatever he had in mind, several 911 calls were placed by those within the firm and a police officer responded immediately: in a town the size of Dalton, it did not take long to get from one part of downtown to another. As the officer arrived on the scene, Cantrell ran around the back of the building, broke out a window, and heaved a homemade bomb into the firm's library on the main floor. The explosion rocked the entire downtown area. The devastation to the building was tremendous, blasting out every window, separating the walls from the foundation, dropping the floor, caving in the basement, and starting a fire that shot upward through the roof. Phillips, who was still negotiating with Cantrell, was blown out of his shoes, his socks melted to his legs. Cantrell himself was killed. Ironically, it was Phillips who had long ago befriended the suicide bomber. Phillips had hired Cantrell to repair his farmhouse; Cantrell had even done work at the firm itself.

Soon two things became clear: what Cantrell intended to accomplish and how catastrophic the event could have been. The man's vehicle was later found packed with canisters of propane, natural gas, and gasoline. If he had succeeded in ramming the building and detonating the bombs inside his SUV, the destruction and injuries would have been much worse. "Put all those ingredients together, and the bomb techs felt like it would have easily reached the buildings surrounding there," said Dalton police chief Jason Parker. "The danger was unfathomable." Authorities surmised that if the vehicle had exploded, then the neighboring post office, apartment building, office building, and elementary school would have suffered massive damage. Scores of people, including schoolchildren across the street, could have been injured or killed.[1]

I was horrified, angered, shocked. Against the protests of my parents, I made immediate plans to fly home. I was told there was nothing I could do: Jim was laid up in a hospital in another city; my father, while shaken, was uninjured; and the building had been condemned by the safety inspector. Cleanup would be impossible until the building was stabilized: we could not even enter to remove files or mementos. I was returning under the auspices of lending a hand in whatever way I could, but in actuality I was returning as much for myself as I was for them. I needed to go to Dalton to lay hands on my father, to wrap my arms around him and make sure he was still intact. I suppose I also wanted to let him know I was glad he was alive.

The next morning, my dad and I, along with some of the

other lawyers and secretaries in the firm, snuck into the building to remove whatever working files were not charred or wet or both. The safety inspector eventually showed up and kicked us out, this time padlocking the building. Seeing the building in ruins, one knew it was a miracle that the only person killed was the bomber himself. I could not believe that my dad, who had been in the records room in the basement, directly beneath the floor where the bomb detonated, had escaped unscathed. The basement was absolutely wrecked.

The bombing affected me as it affected other people from Dalton. It not only personalized the kind of violence that we read about in the headlines or see on the nightly news but also provided an opportunity to reflect. I was not one who courted violence—if anything I went out of my way to avoid it—but the bombing was only the latest in a string of violent episodes that have marked my past in profound and unforgettable ways.

Are my experiences with violence "normal," or at least ordinary in an American context? It's hard to say, and frankly I don't really know, but I suppose that in thinking about how to write this book I have considered my own life as a kind of yardstick, a standard by which to measure norms. As a writer and a scholar, I don't lead a particularly high-risk lifestyle with regard to violence, which is to say I don't regularly find myself in situations where the chances of violence are high. Compared to some, my experiences are undoubtedly quite mild, but I have still had my brushes with violence, my stories to tell. My suspicion is that most of us have firsthand or secondhand stories of violence—that is, we have experienced it directly or know someone who has. If not, then we still get a walloping dose in the local newspaper or on the evening news.

Regardless, one thing seems certain. Violence is everywhere, and it can affect any of us at any time in any place. Horrific violence may touch even the most sheltered individuals in American society. A heavily armed man who worked as a milk-truck driver proved as much on October 2, 2006, when he shot and killed five little girls at West Nickel Mines School, a one-room Amish schoolhouse in Lancaster County, Pennsylvania.[2] It was a dark day, marking an end of innocence for a plain folk working hard to resist not only modern conveniences but also modern dangers, an ugly intrusion on a closed community set on being *in* America without being *of* it. As terrible as that day was for the Pennsylvania Dutch Country, it was an awful day for the rest of the United States too, dispelling whatever illusion of sanctuary still remained in a land of increasingly random violence. If Amish children are not safe at school in rural Pennsylvania, then who is?

For the past ten years I have taught a college course on violence in American culture and society—first as a graduate student instructor at the University of California at Berkeley and then as a professor at Florida Atlantic University. As this course evolved, my students led me to confront the present as much as the past, and what began as a historical overview of political violence, racial violence, labor violence, and war dealt increasingly with more contemporary issues such as cable television, video games, school shootings, and gun control. In trying to understand, we felt as if we were taking the first step toward creating change and making a difference.

Each time I taught the course something terrible seemed to happen, awful events that made our classroom discussions uncomfortably pertinent. More often than not, our in-class deliberations paralleled outside events that made our conversations intensely relevant, each lecture and discussion emphatically punctuated by real-world violence. School shootings recurred with painful regularity: in Pearl, Mississippi (two killed, seven wounded) and in West Paducah, Kentucky (three killed, five wounded) in 1997; in Littleton, Colorado (fifteen killed, twenty-three wounded) in 1999; in Santee, California (two killed, thirteen wounded) in 2001; in Cold Spring, Minnesota (two killed) in 2003; and in Red Lake, Minnesota (ten killed) in 2005. There were so many school shootings—and mall shootings and workplace shootings—that I lost track of them in even-numbered years, when I was not teaching the course. Then as if on cue, as students prepped for final exams in the last days of the Spring 2007 semester, tragedy again struck—this time in Blacksburg, Virginia, where an undergraduate gunned down thirty-two other students before shooting himself. Again, our academic pursuits took on an immediacy that some scholars chase, that many shun, and that few can conjure on their own. It became increasingly important to share with a wider audience what I had learned alongside my students. The result is this book.

Neither a moralist nor a libertarian, neither a pacifist nor a "gun nut," I consider myself a concerned moderate—someone who has not only researched violence in the United States for more than a decade but also worked closely with college students to think creatively about new solutions to old problems. In doing so I have come to see two clear and present dangers: the heightening level of violence around us and our heightening indifference to it. The second danger, of course, often makes us unwilling or unable to confront the first. In the aftermath of bombings or school shootings, we are forced to confront this first danger, but more often than not we return to our well-worn patterns of life after the media furor dies down. We tend to survive from incident to incident, safely inured from the violence until our television sets again make it impossible to ignore—or until it rudely intrudes on our own lives, touching us personally and permanently.

Part of the difficulty in confronting these dual dangers, I think, is that we have been asking the Wrong Questions:

1. Is violence natural, genetically encoded somehow—part of the human condition?
2. Is watching violence harmful to children?
3. Do violent video games produce violent behavior in young people?
4. Is there a causal relation between the number of guns and the levels of violence in our society?
5. Does the Constitution protect not only the right of individual citizens to bear arms but also violent representations in the media?

The Right Questions, I believe, are as follows:

1. How do notions of masculinity affect violent behavior?
2. How harmful is watching violence to any viewer, regardless of age?
3. Does virtual violence enable real violence in ways we may not understand?

4. Is there a correlation between the number of guns and the levels of violence in our society? In other words, how *might* the prevalence of guns in American society heighten levels of violence?
5. If maintaining the public welfare impinges on certain constitutional freedoms, then how does one insure public safety?

This book explores all of these questions, focusing on key themes such as masculinity, entertainment, electronic media, and guns. In addition to reviving words and phrases such as *televiolence* and *gun crazy*, it also introduces a few that may help us to think about violence in new ways.

The introduction presents the notion of *viosense*, inviting the reader to "think violence." Chapter 1 discusses violence as a male phenomenon, covering biological and cultural theories of aggression as related to sex and gender. Chapter 2 deals mainly with violence in movies, television, and video games; it covers research on electronic media violence, public policy, imitation and copycat violence, how seeing violence may help or harm the viewer, and distinctions between real and fantasy violence. Chapter 3 concerns guns: the culture, history, sporting uses, and entertainment value of them, as well as gun violence and related statistics, kids and guns, gun control, and public health. Chapter 4 examines the American fascination with violence—including what I call the *combat culture*—and the problems inherent in normalizing violence. Finally, in rethinking violence, the conclusion suggests a few ways to reduce violence in American society.

When I first began to write this manuscript, I envisioned a book divided into three sections entitled "Real," "Imagined," and "In-Between." The first section would discuss real phenomena in American society—crime, guns, and so forth. The second section would treat fictive, two-dimensional violence in film and television, and the third section would explore the connections between the first two. The more I wrote and the more I tried to organize my thinking, the more I realized that such tidy categories would not work. Violence in the real world feeds violence in Hollywood, which—as its pundits and practitioners constantly remind us—reflects the world in which it exists; however, we also know that the media does not merely reflect the surrounding world. It sculpts, molds, and creates it, existing in constant dialogue with the real.

The French theorist Jean Baudrillard has described a postmodern world of simulation in which identities are constructed by the appropriation of images, in which simulacra (or representations of authenticity masquerading as the real thing) determine how individuals perceive themselves and relate to other people, and in which the hyperreality of entertainment and information technologies overrides the codes and models that structure everyday life. And here was my first breakthrough: insofar as movies (or television shows or video games) affect behavior in the real world—or more accurately, affect attitudes about how one should act or respond in the real world—then movies are as "real" as anything else. St. Augustine recognized as much sixteen centuries ago, when he asserted that seeing interpersonal violence, even simulated violence, is akin to a "stabbing of the soul." Dramatic violence should therefore occur *ob scena* ("offstage," in Latin); such violence, even if necessary to advance the plot, was obscene, unworthy of viewing by the audience. If witnessing violence involves a kind of psychic trauma, as Augustine argued, then perhaps it makes little sense to differentiate between real and imagined violence when considering the effects of both on human health. As this notion turned in my head, the categories "Real," "Imagined," and "In Between" fell away, and I began to see a bigger picture, a way to discuss both violence and representations of violence together. The result is a messier, more complicated analysis, but one that I think is ultimately more accurate and truthful.[3]

Of interest to me is the American ethos of violence—how beliefs, customs, ideals, and practices reinforce and reward violence at all levels of social interaction in this society. Accordingly, this book attempts to consider violence in American culture and society writ large. Of particular interest are the junctures where media violence, entertainment, guns, and notions of manhood intersect; therefore, this book treats all of these subjects in an attempt to find connections, correlations, and interrelated causes. In discussing these topics, it widens the lens as much as possible to get a panoramic view of violence in the United States. It is not intended to exhaust any single area; there are other works, such as Douglas Gentile's *Media Violence and Children* (2003) or Gregg Lee Carter's *The Gun Control Movement* (1997), that perform that function better. Rather, it aims to examine how steeped in violence we really are and to question whether this need be so.

Discussions of violence often revolve around street crime or the violence visited upon us by foreign terrorists, but it seems important to note that violence usually manifests itself much differently in this society. As often as not, violence comes from the familiar, not from outside "others." Our own beliefs and social structures often create violence that eclipses what gangbangers and terrorists wreak, and because I am interested in ethos—the everydayness of violence—my concern lies less with those who define themselves outside the social compact (and for whom society already has a range of criminological and institutional answers) and more with the rest of us: the school kid with his hand balled into a fist, the young man with something to prove, the stockbroker compelled to carry a gun in his glove compartment, the angry husband. With regard to violence, many crimes are committed by average folks, not hardened criminals or political zealots. When regular people with a target and a means of aggressing are momentarily instigated, violence can and does occur. Altering that calculus just a little—minimizing the opportunity or means to aggress, decreasing the tendency for impulsive reaction, removing weapons from the equation, reducing the chance of permanent harm, making violence an unattractive option, or simply giving pause—can change the tipping point and reduce the chances of lethal outcome.

While a large part of this book deals with guns as instruments of violence, I should probably note that I don't find guns detestable. On the contrary, I've gotten a great deal of enjoyment from them. While I don't hunt, I have done and still do a fair amount of shooting—mainly in the vicinity of old soda cans. As a boy, I spent many pleasurable afternoons tossing cans into the Oostanaula River, which ran through a portion of my cousin's farm in North Georgia. I tried to sink them with my .22 rifle, plinking away until the punctured cans disappeared into the muddy water. I pored over gun magazines and as soon as I was legally able, on my twenty-first birthday, purchased a .22 revolver, a Ruger New Model Single-Six (a "fantasy gun," according to Joan Burbick)—in part because I understood owning a handgun as a rite of passage.[4]

I freely admit it: I was seduced by the gun. I know the remorseless facts about guns—the accidental shootings, the suicides, the homicides, the school and workplace shootings, et cetera—and I don't subscribe to the contorted arguments justifying their unregulated ownership and use. I know enough to know how dangerous they are and deep down I suspect that we'd be better off, societally speaking, without them. But— perhaps inexplicably, knowing what I know—I still find them alluring.

Nor do I think violent video games, movies, or TV shows are morally reprehensible, at least not solely because of content. More often I find them reprehensible for their ability to suck time and eat up entire afternoons. I have gleefully and unapologetically played such games as *Grand Theft Auto: Vice City*, *Max Payne*, and *Unreal Tournament*—a first-person-shooter that rewards "head shots"—for hours on end. I have watched *Pulp Fiction* more times than I care to admit, and whatever guilt I have felt in watching the Ultimate Fighting Championship has usually faded after the first flurry of bare-knuckled blows. Does all of this make me a bad person? A hypocrite? Perhaps . . . or maybe it just makes me American. On any given day, like most of us, I am unaware of the cognitive dissonance. On other days, I am unremorseful, even defiant: you can have my joystick when you pry it from my cold dead fingers. However, while I remain comparatively untroubled about guns or video games or violent films on their own, I do confess a growing unease about how these elements freely combine in our society, and toward what end. Are their ill effects cumulative or do they actually catalyze into something different—a new and dangerous toxin born of other chemicals in the environment? I have only recently begun to understand and appreciate how they may potentiate one another like a bad combination of drugs to create unhealthy levels of violence. I harbor a special concern about how these ingredients interact with American notions of masculinity in a way that exacerbates violent outcomes.

My own encounters with violence have surely colored my

views on the subject, and I have tried to be forthright in describing them, as in the opening description of the suicide bombing at my father's workplace. I include them in the interest of full disclosure, to allay any curiosity about my background and how it may have influenced my perspectives. People expect objectivity from college professors and I have done my best to remain professorial; at the same time, I have definite opinions born of assiduous research, careful reflection, and, yes, personal experience. If I have done my job correctly, as a scholar, then whatever biases I have should not be readily apparent; if I have done it honestly, as a writer and as a person, then whatever biases I have should be apparent to all. It is my paradoxical hope to have done my job both correctly and honestly.

A few acknowledgments are in order. Eli Bortz guided this manuscript to Vanderbilt University Press, where the editors, managers, associates, and staff moved it into production with professionalism and speed. I appreciate their commitment and support. Jessie Hunnicutt, the former managing editor at VUP, copyedited the manuscript and made indispensable suggestions for improvement. Thanks also to the librarians at the John D. MacArthur Campus Library of Florida Atlantic University who make my work a little easier; Diane Arrieta, Marilee Brown, William Howerton, Ricardo Pasos, and Ethan Allen, among others, always come through in the clutch.

As already indicated, I am indebted to my students in AMS 4932. This book is an outgrowth of my preparations for this rather unique course. While various studies have explored the subject of violence from psychological, historical, sociological, criminological, and even biological perspectives, it has always been my aim to tackle the study of violence from an interdisciplinary perspective. It is a big topic requiring numerous entry points, and my students have led the way in finding them.

I would also like to thank my family, friends, and colleagues for their support, encouragement, and advice. Mark Tunick, Sallie Brown, and Hasan Jeffries deserve thanks for reading drafts and partial drafts. Jeffrey Goldstein reviewed this manuscript and made invaluable comments, setting me straight on a number of issues. David Griffith deserves special thanks for helping me not only to conceptualize weighty ideas but also to craft my writing skills. Both Goldstein and Griffith have served as models of what thoughtful, socially engaged scholars can create and accomplish, and I would be happy if this book imparted only a fraction of what their writings have taught me. My parents, Dan and Jean Strain, have provided constant support, as always.

Finally, my wife, Melanie, has been extremely patient as I have logged many hours scowling at my computer monitor, and she deserves recognition for a number of intellectual and material contributions. She has provided time and space to think and write, and the debates we have had have strengthened the manuscript. Additionally, and not least importantly, I might have wasted away had she not fed me during especially intense periods of writing. Her love sustains in many ways.

While all of these people and more have contributed to the making of this book, any errors or limitations of style herein are my own.

Reload

Introduction: Thinking Violence

> The idea of living in a society plagued
> by violence is so unappealing that
> Americans tend to hide away from facing
> this thought just as they try to run away
> from specific threats of aggression.
> —Robert Brent Toplin, *Unchallenged
> Violence* (1975)

Outside Looking In

On Monday, April 16, 2007, a student at Virginia Tech opened fire on his classmates and in doing so initiated the deadliest shooting rampage in American history. Cho Seung-Hui, a senior English major, was responsible for two separate shootings on the university campus in Blacksburg, Virginia. The first shooting occurred around 7:15 a.m., when he shot and killed two students at West Ambler Johnston Dormitory. More than two hours later, after an unsuccessful lockdown, Cho shot and killed thirty others across campus at Norris Hall, a science and engineering building whose doors the gunman had chained shut. Witnesses described scenes of mass chaos and unimaginable horror as some students were lined up against a wall and shot while others jumped out of windows to escape. Cho eventually shot himself. Thirty-three people died in all.[1]

Because he killed and injured so many victims in a short span of time, news analysts surmised that Cho had used a semiautomatic assault rifle or perhaps even a fully automatic machine gun. Many were surprised to learn that he had armed himself with two pistols: a 9mm Glock 17 and a .22 Walther P-22. Some wondered whether Cho used after-market, high-capacity, thirty-three-round Glock magazines available for purchase in Virginia. Investigators quickly traced the two guns to a legal sale at a gun shop in nearby Roanoke. Cho apparently bought his first gun, the Glock, on March 13; the gun came with two fifteen-round magazines. He purchased the Walther the week before the shooting. Because Virginia law prohibits buying more than one handgun in a thirty-day period, Cho waited the full month before buying the Walther. As an alien with a green card, the twenty-three-year-old was able to buy handguns legally as long as he provided proof of his residence—which he did. The shop owner, John Markell, told reporters that there was nothing unusual about the transactions. Markell said that in eight years of running his store he had sold approximately sixteen thousand guns. Of those, four had been used in homicides and two in suicides.[2]

The following day NBC News broadcast material sent to its television studios in New York by the gunman. In his videotaped manifesto, Cho glorified the 1999 Columbine High School shooters, Eric Harris and Dylan Klebold. In a series of still photographs also sent to NBC, he seemed to strike poses copied from *Oldboy*, a gory, ultraviolent South Korean revenge film that won the Grand Jury Prize at the 2004 Cannes Film Festival.[3]

College campuses far from Blacksburg flew their flags at half-staff and conducted memorial services. A nation grieved. Like Columbine, the tragedy in Blacksburg again awakened Americans to the possibility that a criminal-minded individual with a gun could visit wrathful, lethal violence upon unsuspecting citizens anywhere—in this locality or that one, at *their* school or workplace. The unspoken realization among collegians, educators, and students nationwide was that *it could have happened here, it could have happened to us*.

The shooting conjured up all sorts of emotions as the nation mourned, deeply and profoundly. Americans were shocked, horrified, saddened, enraged—sometimes in stages, sometimes all at once. People around the world grieved with us, but the range of emotional responses abroad included other sentiments too. "Expressions of sympathy rang out from Buckingham Palace to Beijing as the world absorbed the news of yet another deadly shooting spree in the United States," reported *USA Today*. "But the Virginia Tech massacre also heightened questions about how such horrific violence could break out with such regularity in America, and whether relatively lax U.S. gun laws are not a case of freedom gone too far." While there was widespread shock internationally, few foreigners expressed surprise, and some expressed a kind of embarrassment, an emotion that few Americans registered.[4]

Newspapers in London viewed the event with incredulity. "Only the Names Change," ran a headline in the *Times*, "and the Numbers." With America's unrestrictive gun laws and propensity for everyday violence, "even school shootings were in danger of being treated as commonplace," reported the *Daily Mail*. "How Many More?" ran another headline in the same paper. "Isn't it incredible that after all this," the article reported, "vast numbers of Americans still resist every attempt to introduce sensible gun control laws? . . . There is a huge amount to admire about the U.S. and its people. But the crazed killers are not the only ones who need their heads examined."[5]

An American, the father of a sixteen-year-old high school student in New York, wrote a commentary in still another article in the *Daily Mail*:

> The awful, even revolting, truth is that as a parent in America you simply cannot take it for granted when you wave your children off on the yellow school bus in the morning that they will come safely home again. . . . We need security against terrorism in air travel, but why at school? . . . The nation which once slung on its six-guns to rescue Europe and the world from the horrors of totalitarianism and genocide now resembles the bad guy straddling the world like Tony Soprano looking for business in a gang war. . . . It is symbolic that Virginia, scene of yesterday's tragedy, is at the epicenter of American gun culture. How proud that makes the National Rifle Association! The old Virginie Colony of George Washington is still armed to the teeth, ready to reach under the bed for the gun to bring justice to that arrogant King George.

The author concluded with a reference to the war in Iraq: "The nation which believes it can create democracy and market economies at will, along the trade routes of the world, should be able to control its own domestic gun market."[6]

In a separate article, the *Daily Mail* concluded, "Despite repeated school shootings, it is still ridiculously easy to obtain a gun in the U.S." The *Daily Telegraph* credited the "muscular pro-gun lobby" with warding off restrictions; resting on the Second Amendment, America's gun lobby "has become almost unassailable."[7] One writer for the *Guardian* observed,

> The response of many who wish America ill will has been gratuitous *schadenfreude*. They see a people who live by the gun also dying by it, be they marines in Anbar province or students in Virginia. . . . Britons whose links with America are long and close (and in my case familial) always find themselves pleading the same cause. First, we scrupulously proclaim the standing of America as a world exemplar of political freedom, though this has become a sort of Hail Mary, recited before yet another pro/anti-American argument. Then we beg Americans to step outside their continent and see themselves as others do. . . . More American children (some 3000) may die by gunfire each year than the death toll on 9/11, far more than in any other developed country. This may be a function of a migratory society or an unstable community, though it is hard to dissociate it from lax gun laws.

"When politicians lack courage," the writer concluded, "policy goes wrong and someone dies. It is as simple as that." The *Financial Times* explored responses to the tragedy by American politicians, who "raced to voice their horror" at what happened. "But if history is anything to go by," the paper reported, "expressions of outrage will lead to little in terms of tighter gun control."[8]

Other papers across Great Britain echoed the London dailies. "America has stopped once again to take a long hard look at itself and a culture in which many ordinary people are said to feel they are not safe without a rifle under the bed and a revolver in the glovebox," reported the *Yorkshire Post*, which surmised that the American zeal for firearms "stems from the decision of the Founding Fathers more than 200 years ago to enshrine in the U.S. Constitution the right for individuals 'to keep and bear arms' rather than any pragmatic concern for the growing prevalence of firearms in a modern society."[9] Scottish newspapers expressed similar concerns. "We'll never know why, but we do know how," wrote the *Scottish Daily Record and Sunday Mail*. "America's relaxed gun laws make it too easy for the wicked, the desperate, the deranged to fulfill their warped fantasies." Glasgow's *Herald* described the antiquated marriage of Americans to guns and their inability to prevent shooting sprees as "the politics of madness and despair," while the *Aberdeen Press and Journal* explained to its readers, "Guns are to Americans what umbrellas are to Scots." The paper wondered, "Nobody ever explains why Americans carry guns as if they were pocket handkerchiefs. It's not as if there were still wild frontiers to be conquered." Irish papers relayed identical accounts and opinion pieces. "Gun violence may cost $2.3 billion each year in medical expenses, but that too, gun supporters believe, is a price worth paying to protect a fundamental freedom," reported the *Irish Independent*. "Even to an America numbed by numerous school shootings," wrote the *Belfast Telegraph*, "the massacre at Virginia Tech has plumbed appalling new depths."[10]

The British response reflected a different perspective on such tragedies. It is not that the Brits were not equally horrified by the deaths in Blacksburg or that they did not empathize with us Yanks in our time of sorrow. It is that they truly did not understand how such events continued to happen without any kind of behavioral modification or public policy change on the part of American citizens or their elected officials. To non-Americans, such events seem so preventable, so avoidable; to us they seem inescapable, obligatory.

The editorial response of British newspapers also recalled the United Kingdom's own tough battles in restricting firearms. British guns laws, among the world's toughest, stemmed directly from two particular shooting sprees. In August 1987, twenty-seven-year-old Michael Ryan, armed with a semiautomatic AK-47, a Beretta pistol, and a fragmentation grenade, killed sixteen people and wounded fifteen others. Parliament subsequently banned semiautomatic and pump-action center-fire rifles. In March 1996, Thomas Hamilton shot dead sixteen young children and their teacher at the primary school in

Dunblane, a small Scottish town. As a result of the Dunblane shooting, handguns were outlawed in 1997 in Britain; some 160,000 were surrendered to police. It is a strict law—even the national Olympic pistol-shooting team, barred from practicing on British soil, must train outside the country—but the result is dramatic: Britain's 46 homicides involving firearms in 2006 was the lowest since the late 1980s. (New York City, with eight million people compared to fifty-three million in England and Wales, recorded 579 homicides in 2006—and New York City has tight gun control laws, by U.S. standards).[11]

Other newspapers in other parts of the world seemed perplexed by the antediluvian prescriptions of the U.S. Constitution, particularly the Second Amendment. "Never mind if that clause was drawn up in another era—when communities needed guns to hunt and to protect themselves from highwaymen—which would probably be unrecognizable to modern Americans," wrote the *Hindustan Times* in New Delhi. Similarly a contributor to the *New Zealand Herald* wrote, "At the time when Americans were given the right to bear arms, black people were slaves and women couldn't vote." In a separate article the paper wrote, "Non-Americans may be amazed, but a state law in the 1990s limiting handgun purchases to one per person per month was seen as a step towards curbing Virginia's reputation as a source of easily acquired weapons." A Japanese translator and essayist named Hirokai Sato discovered a startling fact in New York while checking figures provided by the Centers for Disease Control and Prevention (CDC): the number of people murdered in Blacksburg—thirty-two—was in fact the daily average for killings by firearms in the United States.[12]

Tim Kaine, the Democratic governor of Virginia, returned early from a trip to Japan and declared a state of emergency, which enabled him to deploy resources to Blacksburg quickly. At a Tuesday evening news conference, he answered a reporter's question about students carrying guns on campus by stating, "People who want to take this within twenty-four hours and make it their political hobby horse to ride, I've got nothing but loathing for them." He would later create an eight-member panel to investigate everything from Cho's mental health to the response of school officials; the panel report, released four months later, would fault school administrators for not better alerting the campus community as the incident unfolded.[13] Meanwhile, President George W. Bush offered his prayers. "We hold the victims in our hearts," he said in a press release on Monday, "and we ask a loving God to comfort those who are suffering today." The president spoke at a memorial service at Virginia Tech the day after the shooting, and commissioned the secretary of health and human services, the secretary of education, and the attorney general to investigate "issues raised by the Virginia Tech tragedy"; the result was a weak report recommending better communication between state and federal agencies, better implementation of pre-existing programs, and better diagnosis of mental illness.[14]

What did not occur in the aftermath reveals more perhaps than what did. Even in the face of such a tragedy, the Democratic governor and the Republican president hesitated to call for gun control, and this hesitation speaks volumes not only about the depth of the nation's commitment to gun owning but also about American attitudes toward violence. Rather than a debate about guns, the Virginia Tech massacre prompted a debate about campus security. Virginia Tech, along with other colleges across the nation, began the 2007–2008 school year with new electronic keypads and increased campus surveillance. Had Americans somehow been able to escape the horror of the moment and see it as others living outside the United States saw it, we might have responded differently. Instead, school officials sanctioned more metal detectors in college buildings, as groups such as Students for Concealed Carry on Campus championed arming students in the classroom.[15]

Getting Perspective

The response of the international press to what happened in Blacksburg might alert us to the customariness of violence in American life. Violence is universal, ancient, and omnipresent, existing worldwide across different societies throughout human history. War, revolution, political violence, and assassinations all predate the modern era; yet, a kind of purposeless violence—violence for its own sake—has thrived in our own times, particularly in our own nation, in such a way as to become almost unremarkable. To Americans it can seem quite normal when in fact it is anything but normal, and this unremarkableness is itself quite remarkable.

It is not that Americans do not empathize when human life is lost. Shortly after the Virginia Tech killings, the I-35W bridge collapse in Minnesota in which twelve people died and the Crandall Canyon mine collapse in Utah in which six miners (plus three rescuers) lost their lives both garnered comparable media attention, generating an outpouring of sympathy in August 2007. Accidents, however, differ from shooting sprees, and for whatever reason, the *taking* of human life, as opposed to the loss of it, has lost much of its shock value. Violent crimes and murders—quite commonplace in our news media—capture our attention only when particularly vile or vicious. While still front-page news, they threaten to become routine, the journalistic equivalents of fender benders.

Images of violence are numbingly customary in this society—difficult, in fact, to escape. We get a steady dose of violence in the local newspaper, in the theater, and online. It is a staple ingredient in television programming. It laces our news, and we often seek it in our sports and entertainment. People living in the United States are surrounded by violence, whether random or intentional, real or simulated, serious or "fun." Perhaps the familiarity of such images has desensitized us, making it easy to take such violence for granted. But there are reminders, some not so subtle, that violence is not a universal human behavior.

Statistics indicate shocking discrepancies between the United States and other nations, revealing just how violent a place the United States really is. According to the Justice Department, the homicide rate declined in the United States from a spike of 10.5 per 100,000 in 1991 to 6.1 in 2000 (the lowest rate since 1967); by comparison, according to the World Health Organization, the homicide rates in France, Germany, and Great Britain in 2000 were 0.6, 0.8, and 0.9, respectively. Children in the United States are far more likely to be shot and killed than their counterparts in other industrial nations; the firearms homicide rate is sixteen times higher for American children. As alarming as such numbers may be, it is the U.S.

homicide rate involving handguns that makes the United States stand apart internationally. In 1996, for example, handguns were used to murder 30 people in Great Britain, 106 in Canada, 15 in Japan, and 9,390 in the United States. The CDC reports the rate of firearms deaths (that is, the number of Americans shot to death per 100,000) as hovering between 8.8 and 9.2 for white Americans during the period 2000–2005, between 7.5 and 7.8 for Hispanic or Latino Americans, and between 18.4 and 19.3 for African Americans. Such statistics suggest that there is something unique—and frightening—happening in the United States.[16]

Of course, the homicide rate is only one yardstick by which to measure violence. It is the most easily quantifiable index, the most visible phenomenon—but there is a great deal of aggressive behavior that is not so extreme. It might help to think of homicide as the tip of the iceberg—not only because it is the most readily identifiable indicator of violence but also because it heralds an immense problem just below the surface of American life. For example, there were thirty-five school killings in the United States in 1998—a horrific enough number on its own—but two psychologists who study child development recently reported that for every school killing there were over 7,000 serious injuries, 28,000 thefts, 44,000 physical altercations, and 500,000 reports of bullying in American schools. These numbers, of course, reflect *reported* incidents of violent behavior; the actual number of incidents was presumably far higher.[17]

Teachers and educators have reported that schoolchildren have become more disrespectful, more verbally aggressive, and more likely to push and shove each other in recent years. With this violence come a hardened use of weaponry and a stony lack of compassion. Some kids are willing to shoot not only adversaries but also bystanders, as evidenced by the nineteen-year-old who shot into a school bus full of children, wounding an eight-year-old boy in Shreveport in March 2006, and the seventeen-year-old who fired five times at rival gang members on a school bus in West Las Vegas in September 2006.[18] Equally disturbing are the recent spate of assaults by teenagers on the nation's homeless population. The National Coalition for the Homeless, an advocacy group based in Washington, D.C., reports that there were 472 attacks on homeless people, including 169 deaths, from 1999 to 2005; the year 2006 recorded the most in a decade, with 122 attacks and 20 murders. In March 2007, youths set a man ablaze in Boston as he slept in a park, and another man's beating by teens was captured by video cameras at a store in San Francisco. In January 2007, three young men attacked Norris Gaynor, who had been sleeping on a park bench in Fort Lauderdale. The three chased Gaynor and beat him to death with a baseball bat; surveillance cameras at Florida Atlantic University captured part of the beating. Shooting into a crowd of people or brutalizing someone who is already down on his or her luck are part of what some cultural critics have identified as a larger "culture of disrespect," or the "triumph of meanness" in American society.[19]

If there is meanness at work in American society, then youth violence has often been at the center of it. Cultural critics identified this meanness in the 1980s when they bemoaned the state of a society in which one boy would shoot another for his Nike sneakers, a society in which crass materialism and the pursuit of the latest and greatest threatened to overtake everything, even the sanctity of human life itself. Then as now, incidents of youth violence were disturbing because they suggested not only an apparent victory of evil over innocence but also a Faustian bargain with liberal democracy that precluded social welfare: they suggested that even the best intentions of parents, joined with societal safeguards, are incapable of shielding children from the worst aspects of that same society. "Shoejackings" in the 1980s were extra disturbing because they symbolized a perversion of American capitalism carried to foreseeable extremes. It was little comfort to know that these shoejackings had a kind of internal logic: the logic of theft, melded with American acquisition carried to murderous ends. Such incidents signified a culture in danger of losing its center, a culture of greed and skewed priorities; but, as disturbing as such incidents were, in a land of flaunted wealth, frozen opportunities, precarious status, and casual violence they came as little surprise.[20]

If shoejackings carried a kind of twisted logic, then there has been nothing logical about the school shootings that have plagued the United States over the past several decades. Few incidents capture the sense of a world gone mad like these. For example, when Brenda Ann Spencer opened fire on children at Cleveland Elementary School in San Diego on January 29, 1979, her actions dramatized the problem of youth violence like nothing else up to that point in American history. Barricaded in her house across the street from the school, the sixteen-year-old girl killed two men while wounding eight students and a police officer. Principal Burton Wragg was attempting to rescue children in the line of fire when he was shot and killed, and custodian Mike Suchar was slain attempting to aid Wragg. Spencer used a rifle her father had given her as a gift. As to why she fired upon the children, the girl explained to a reporter, "I don't like Mondays. . . . This livens up the day." According to a report written by police negotiators who spoke with her during the six-hour standoff, she further elaborated: "There was no reason for it, and it was just a lot of fun. . . . It was just like shooting ducks in a pond. . . . [The children] looked like a herd of cows standing around, it was really easy pickings."[21]

As appalling as the incident was, few people outside of southern California might have remembered the Spencer shooting had it not been immortalized in popular culture by a song. The Irish punk-rock band Boomtown Rats was conducting an interview at a U.S. radio station when the story of Brenda Spencer came over the newswire; later that year, the band recorded what would become its biggest hit, "I Don't Like Mondays." The song's lyrics searched for meaning in the senseless event. Because of lawsuits by the Spencer family and public sensitivity to the issue of gun violence, the song only reached #77 in the Billboard charts even as it became a cult classic.[22]

Spencer was not the first teen killer. Charles Starkweather, for example, was nineteen in 1958 when he led fourteen-year-old Caril Fugate on a weeklong killing spree across Nebraska and Wyoming in which eleven people were shot, stabbed, and strangled to death. In 1966, twenty-four-year-old Charles Whitman—a former Eagle Scout, U.S. Marine, and expert marksman—climbed to the top of the clock tower of the University of Texas at Austin, where he was a junior. Armed with a footlocker full of ammunition, shotguns, rifles, and sandwiches, he sniped forty-six people in an hour and a half, killing sixteen before police killed him. Four months later, eighteen-year-old Robert Benjamin Smith took seven female hostages in a beauty salon in Mesa, Arizona, and fatally shot five of them, including a three-year-old girl. After the police arrived he confessed, telling them he was inspired by Charles Whitman and Richard Speck, who had killed eight student nurses in Chicago that same year. During Christmas break in 1974, eighteen-year-old Anthony Barbaro entered his high school in Olean, New York, and set several fires; when a custodian investigated, Barbaro—a member of the school's rifle team—shot him dead, then fired from a third-floor window at firefighters and passersby, killing two more people and wounding nine.[23]

Twenty-five years later, a pair of shooters blasted into American consciousness, opening a frank dialogue on the phenomenon of school shootings. On April 20, 1999, eighteen-year-old Eric Harris and seventeen-year-old Dylan Klebold entered Columbine High School in Littleton, Colorado, with two sawed-off shotguns, a Hi-Point semiautomatic rifle, and a 9mm Intratec Tec-9, a high-capacity, semiautomatic "assault pistol" popular with street gangs for its firepower and concealability. Having earlier hidden at least thirty pipe bombs and a twenty-five-pound propane bomb throughout the school, the two then proceeded to open fire, shooting thirty-five people before shooting themselves. Twelves students and one teacher died, in addition to the two gunmen. Supplanting the Spencer shooting as the most appalling school shooting in U.S. history, the Columbine attack sent shock waves across the nation, prompted discussions on everything from school safety to mental health, and created a demand for prevention and protection.

Of all the incidents of violence that occur in our society, school shootings are perhaps the most gut-wrenching because of their seeming senselessness, their avoidability. How could children do such things, we ask. If only someone had paid attention, if only someone had listened. Still, the scholastic equivalent of "going postal" continues to occur, as it has for the past fifty years, with increasing frequency and cataclysm.

But kids, of course, are not the only ones acting with brutality. If youth violence is rampant, then so too is adult violence. Consider the widespread incidents of "road rage," a prob-

falo hunters, traders, gamblers, and barflies—represented one extreme with seven men for every woman in 1870, but even agricultural communities such as Richardson County, Nebraska, and Wells County, North Dakota, had notable gender imbalances. Honor, racism, alcohol, moral laxity, vice, guns, and vigilantism were all elements of frontier life, and none of them had a particularly soothing effect on the rough-and-ready frontiersman. The fact that most men were unmarried, existing in a supermasculinized environment without the civilizing presence of women, only made matters worse. Courtwright's Old West is a place of atomized existence, a place where young men—proud and drunk, cocked and loaded like the guns they carried—bumped into one another and blood spilled. *Violent Land* notes many parallels between the wooly frontier of the nineteenth century and the wild frontier of America's inner cities today, where young men sling guns, run drugs, and posture for one another.[4]

Courtwright's thesis is commonsensical and deceptively simple, and *Violent Land* provides a platform from which to launch a discussion of the historical, biological, and cultural dimensions of violence. At the very least, the author makes a strong case for the overwhelmingly male and overwhelmingly youthful nature of criminal violence. "The thefts and outrages of everyday life are most often the opportunistic acts of young men impulsive or undisciplined enough to break the law and strong or quick enough to get away with it," he writes. "Street crime is a young man's game."[5] It is in this volatile mixture of biological and cultural inheritance that American men find easily accessible ideas about using aggression to get what they want. If men are a violent bunch by nature, then what they learn about being men, and how they internalize what their societies teach about masculinity, surely has the potential to make a bad problem worse.

Me Tarzan, You Jane

Of course, Courtwright may overstate the role of nature in men's violent behaviors. It is undeniable that males of all ages are more violent overall than females of comparable ages, and that they are arrested for far more crimes than females; according to Lee Bowker, editor of *Masculinities and Violence* (1998), "Female violent crime is so rare that some states have managed to survive for a century without any prison for women."[6] It is also undeniable that young men in groups can enable one another to participate in increasingly heightened levels of violence. Such truisms do not mean, however, that men are "naturally" more violent than women. It is equally true, for example, that women sometimes model male behavior and are capable of adopting male patterns of aggression—just as a number of men are nurturing, loving, and peaceable, embodying personality traits we tend to attribute to women. How different individuals are socialized, regardless of gender, undoubtedly has a major bearing on whether they express themselves with violence or aggression.

"When other conditions are equal," reports one scholar, "men and women seem to be equally aggressive."[7] If so, then when are such conditions equal, and why do women fail to model violent behavior as often as men? It makes sense to characterize violence as a male phenomenon, not only because so much more violence occurs at the hands of males than of females but also because males are often expected and encouraged to behave violently in certain situations. "Even if boys and girls were born with equal propensities for violence," writes Bowker, "the immense and intense socialization differences between the two genders would cause them to behave very differently."[8] Traditionally, while boys have play-fought and learned to employ aggression, girls—on the other side of the playground—have role-played nonviolently. Both sets of respective behaviors have found favor with those monitoring the children's games: one is boy-play, the other girl-play, and neither is deemed particularly appropriate for the other group. That is, males are typically socialized—as boys, as adolescents, and as men—to be violent. They are not born that way. If testosterone does fuel aggressive behavior at some level, then it usually takes societal input to raise that aggression to the level of violence.

In pinpointing the biological disposition of men to commit violence, scientists privilege what might be called the testosterone factor: the preordained, chemical proclivity of men to behave violently. Men simply cannot help but to act aggressively, according to this theory. It is in our blood, in our DNA. Biological factors make us prone to punch and shoot and wrestle and gouge, but environmental factors—namely a clutch of other men, with similarly jacked-up levels of testosterone—provide a setting for mayhem. If a group of men get together in Courtwright's world without the soothing, civilizing presence of a lady, then all hell will likely break loose.

In considering the testosterone factor, and in considering the merits of Courtwright's thesis, it is important to distinguish between biologically determined sex and culturally constructed gender. Sex typically refers to the anatomical differences between the male and the female of any particular species. Gender refers to the meanings that particular cultures attach to a person's sex. Similarly, manhood refers to the condition of being an adult male, while masculinity refers to those qualities ascribed to being a male. Generally speaking, sex and womanhood and manhood are matters of biology, while gender and femininity and masculinity are matters of culture; the two realms, of course, intersect and affect one another in the complicated process of determining what it means to be a man or a woman. Such distinctions help to explain efforts by academicians who initially looked to sex rather than gender in trying to trace the roots of aggression in human populations.

Aggression and Its Discontents

Anyone who has watched an animal menacingly bare its teeth may have also wondered whether human beings harbor an innate tendency toward violence. The suspicion, investigated by a surprising number of researchers from the nineteenth century to the present, is that men in particular are atavistic brutes, ready to club anyone or anything that does not signal complete submission. If we could prove that men are little more than domesticated animals with feral tendencies, then it would go a long way toward proving scientifically the natural aggressiveness of humankind. Anthropologists, sociologists, criminologists, physiologists, biologists, doctors, psychiatrists, psychologists, political scientists, and historians have all posited theories about human aggression in an attempt to answer the question, "Is violence natural, genetically encoded somehow?" Some have indeed argued that since our animal ancestors were instinctively violent creatures, and since we have evolved from them, we bear the genetic imprint of their violence and act accordingly.[9]

A number of assumptions anchor these traditional bioexplanations of aggression. Confirmed by pioneering studies such as Konrad Lorenz's *On Aggression* (1966), these assumptions have percolated into common thinking on the subject. Many people unquestioningly assume that expressing anger is healthful, that humans are instinctively aggressive, that aggression can be rechanneled into healthy pursuits, that aggressive play is good for children, that domestic abuse results from mental illness, that aggression causes violent crime, that men are biologically predisposed to violence, that emotions are beyond control, that anger fuels aggression, and that war is the logical extreme of aggression.[10]

But other scholars have subsequently questioned these early studies and the assumptions they engendered. Jeffrey Goldstein, for example, undertook a meta-analysis of these studies in his sweeping work *Aggression and Crimes of Violence*, first published in 1975 and updated in 1986. Exploring the empirical research on human aggression and violent crime, Goldstein reviewed over five hundred studies, almost half of which were published between the two editions of his own book. *Aggression and Crimes of Violence* systematically challenged all of the assumptions that informed common thinking on aggression. The author argued that the evidence that higher primates are instinctively aggressive was weak; then he argued that even if we could establish such aggression, it does not logically follow that humans would be aggressive too. "To argue that because we *can* behave like lower organisms, we *must* behave like them is preposterous," he wrote.[11]

In the late 1960s and 1970s criminologists popularized the notion that hyperaggressiveness in males was caused by a genetic abnormality, an extra Y chromosome. These so-called XYY males accounted for approximately 3 percent of violent criminals tested in both maximum-security prisons and mental hospitals. Another explanation, rechanneling, involved a branch of Freudian theory that explained how aggressive energy could be channeled into nonaggressive behavior. All of us have aggressive tendencies, the Freudians argued, but some of us learn to redirect them or bleed them off. But these physiological explanations of aggression have since been scrutinized and largely discredited. Scholars such as Goldstein wondered how hyperaggression might account for the other 97 percent incarcerated for violence who were *not* XYY males; other scholars presented research invalidating catharsis theory, thereby dealing a blow to notions of rechanneling.

Perhaps the most incontrovertible way to refute the single-cause, biological theory of aggression was to show that it is in fact not a universal instinct—that some (albeit few) societies show no overt signs of violence—and indeed, some researchers discovered as much. The British-American anthropologist Ashley Montagu found little or no aggression in the Toda and Birhor peoples of southern India, the Tasaday of Mindanao (in the Philippines), the Punan of Borneo, the Hadza of Tanzania, the Veddahs of Ceylon, the Arapesh of New Guinea, the aboriginal peoples of Australia, the Yamis of Orchid Island (off Taiwan), the Semai of Malaya, the Tikopia of the western Pacific, the Land Dayaks of Sarawak, the Leppchas of Sikkim, the Papago Indians, the Hopi and Zuni and Pueblo peoples of the American Southwest, native Tahitians, and the Ifaluk of the Pacific.[12] If entire groups of people exhibit *no* aggressive tendencies, then aggression would not seem to be a naturally occurring behavior, endemic to the human condition. "That few men do kill or maim others seems to refute the notion of a biological urge or instinct to murder," one government researcher has noted. "Whatever man's aggressive impulses, obviously most men learn to control them."[13]

The implication is clear. If we recognize how societal norms circumscribe certain kinds of behavior, then we might agree that violence is less often a physiological reaction than a cognitive choice. In most situations in which interpersonal violence is possible, an individual weighs consequences and decides that naked aggression would be either too costly or inappropriate; in this way conflict is avoided through nonviolent means. We might call this decision-making process the calculus of violence. A person must decide how upset or angered he really is, how he would justify a violent response to others, how he would justify a violent response to himself, and so forth. These processes are rational and cognitive, not emotive or instinctual; as such, they moderate whatever "natural" tendency one has to aggress.

To ask whether violence is natural is to ask whether people are predisposed to act violently; however, to ask this question is also to privilege genetic hardwiring over child rearing, gender modeling, and socialization in determining violent behavior. In some sense, it is the wrong question because hormones, testosterone, and the Y-chromosome probably have less to do with violent behavior than do our beliefs about how we ought to act in a given situation. Otherwise, we would clobber one another much more often than we already do, and we would not be far removed from other animals, scrapping for survival. As it is, culture not only works in concert with biology to affect how we function but also usually overrides it in social settings. People have the ability to reason, and reason trumps instinct more often than not in daily human interactions, circumscribed by social mores. For example, we typically subscribe to certain societal norms in determining whether we walk on the right-hand side of the sidewalk, whether we remove our hats at the dinner table, and whether we shake hands when we greet. We similarly subscribe to certain societal norms when we decide whether or not to ram someone who cuts us off in traffic or to punch a belligerent drunk in a bar.

Today, researchers of all sorts recognize the interaction between hormonal and genetic factors and environmental influences and triggers. Saying that violence is either biological or learned is a false dichotomy, but the readiness to ascribe violent tendencies solely to natural impulse still lingers. In sum, three related points bear mention. First, the testosterone factor, which lies at the heart of most biological explanations of aggression, can obscure the fact that what it means to be a man or woman is at least in part a human invention. Second, whether men are naturally violent or not matters less from a prescriptive standpoint than whether our culture enables or encourages violence in various ways. The former we have little control over; the latter, while formidable, offers some measure of reform. In fact, we should probably be thankful that biological explanations of aggression only partially explain what they attempt to analyze. To accept an aggression-instinct hypothesis would lead us to an unquestioning acceptance of aggression, crime, violence, and war as inevitable, and accepting these behaviors as inevitable places us either in a passive position with respect to eradicating such behaviors or in the position of eugenicists, attempting to control violence through repression or selective breeding. Neither position is savory. Third and finally, to argue for a broader cultural explanation of aggression and violence is not to deny the limits that biology sets on human behavior; it is instead to see how complex and multicausal violence actually is, to appreciate how culture seeps into our very beings to affect who we are and what we do.

Men, American Style

To recognize masculinity as a human invention is to recognize it as a historical phenomenon, culturally circumscribed. Ideas about masculinity transform over time, changing like fashion from generation to generation. In the closing years of the nineteenth century, for example, ambition and combativeness became virtues for American men in a new way; competitiveness and aggression were exalted as ends in themselves. Toughness was admired and tenderness scorned, and perhaps no one embodied these qualities better than President Theodore Roosevelt, whose 1899 speech "The Strenuous Life" called American men to test themselves through adversity. Strength, appearance, and athletic skill mattered more in the Victorian era than in previous centuries. Throughout the twentieth century, American men operated in accordance with these virtues, and they continue to do so today—largely because such notions are a part of our cultural inheritance.

However, as E. Anthony Rotundo has demonstrated in *American Manhood: Transformations in Masculinity from the Revolution to the Modern Era* (1993), this reverence for ambition and combativeness itself grew out of earlier American notions of manhood that privileged virtue and moderation over ruthlessness in the name of winning. After tracing the evolution of manhood in nineteenth-century America, the author concludes,

> We have all learned a set of cultural types—the tough man and the tender, the real man and the sissy that have been accumulating cultural sanction for over a century now. These types, or symbols, encourage males to value certain kinds of men and to scorn others. This process harms men who fit the wrong type. Less directly, it harms *all* men because they lose access to stigmatized parts of themselves—tenderness, nurturance, the desire for connection, the skills of cooperation—that are helpful in personal situations and needed for the social good.[14]

If modern American masculinity models certain philistine characteristics, then it is nice to know that it has not always been so—and, perhaps, that it need not be so. Indeed, the author reminds us that gender roles in American history have changed over time, evolving with the growth of the American republic. Rotundo's scholarship provides a baseline for understanding the fluidity of gender while explaining why American men are what they are.

Certainly, the construction of masculinity offers keys to understanding male-patterned behavior, particularly violent behavior. All manner of aggressive behaviors—from disagreements, quarrels, and arguments to fights, feuds, and wars—transpire because men are searching for manly responses to particular conflicts. Externally informed notions of manhood, therefore, inform male actions; oftentimes these responses are neither justifiable nor judicious, neither calculated nor intentional. One need look no further than the stands of a football stadium or the stools of a sports bar to know that much jackassery takes place in the name of manliness.

American men indeed go to great lengths to avoid the label "wimp," and the not-so-comical contortions that arise in disassociating oneself from this label sometimes have repercussions far beyond one's reputation. For example, in *The Wimp Factor: Gender Gaps, Holy Wars, and the Politics of Anxious Masculinity* (2004), psychotherapist Stephen Ducat describes the creation of gender and how it influences political and religious discourses. Masculinity is, surprisingly, very fragile. "For many men," he writes, "masculinity is a hard-won, yet precarious and brittle psychological achievement that must be constantly proven and defended." Such fragile masculinities, camouflaged as real manhood, often drive conservative political agendas and fundamentalist religious beliefs, according to the author. Ducat defines not only "femiphobia"—the fear of women—but also what he calls "anxious masculinity," or a paralyzing dread by men of the "feminine" within them; both share a dangerous kind of misogyny. The problem is not men, per se; in other words, there is nothing pathological about being male, according to Ducat. "Rather, the problem is the psychological cost of developing a male identity in a culture that disparages the feminine," he writes, "and insists that the boundaries between masculine and feminine remain unambiguous and impermeable."[15]

For example, Ducat sees "many of the most vivid expressions of men's fears" in the "colorful vernacular of everyday macho invective": labels such as *mama's boy*, *girly-man*, *nancy*, *pansy*, *bitch*, *punk*, *fag*, *queer*, *sissy*, *wimp*, *pussy*, and the creative combination *wussy*. Such language serves to denigrate both women and homosexual men simultaneously. "These terms of hypermasculine derision attest to the narrow and rigid boundaries in which our prevailing notions of maleness are confined," he writes. "Such words also tell us much about the shame that results from the failure to remain within these constricting borders."[16]

As human beings, we understand gender in a certain social and cultural context. More commonly, however, we understand gender (as we do sex) through comparison; for example, we understand masculinity in terms of its contrast with femininity. Over and over again, in different societies around the world, the most important thing about being a man is not being a woman. The United States is no different in this regard: what is different, perhaps, is the way such notions have come to dominate political discourse. Ducat convincingly demonstrates how right-wing political propagandists have, since the 1980 national election, "relentlessly and with great success linked liberalism to weakness, dependency, and helplessness—qualities seen by most male-dominant societies as feminine."[17] Consequently, American men have often reacted negatively to social welfare programs such as subsidized child care and food stamps since their effective implementation in the 1960s.

One need look no further than the new alignments in political contests to see the gendered nature of American electoral politics: "soccer moms," "office park dads," "security moms," and "NASCAR dads" are now seen as the demographic groups that decide elections. Accordingly, political candidates must assert themselves in unmistakably gendered ways. "Even a relatively liberal presidential candidate, John Kerry, in November of 2003 felt compelled to drag reporters and an AP photographer to a chilly field in Iowa, the first caucus state in the Democratic primary, to watch him blow pheasants away with his twelve-gauge shotgun," Ducat notes. "Apparently, Mr. Kerry wanted to reassure the male electorate that even though he supports a ban on assault weapon sales, he still likes to kill things."[18]

Noting that George H. W. Bush had to fight the "wimp factor" throughout his presidency, and that his son's actions may be interpreted as attempts to "remasculate" his father (and himself), Ducat provides insightfully devastating psychological profiles of both Presidents Bush. The elder Bush "had failed to counter the popular view of himself as a pampered patrician, a man of effete and precious sensibilities whose road through life had always been smoothed by inherited wealth and nepotistic advantage—all qualities that have been coded feminine in American political culture for centuries," he writes.[19] Not to be mistaken for anything other than a man's man, George W. Bush, born with a silver spoon in his mouth, adopted the ways of the quintessential American male archetype, the Texas cowboy:

> One can only speculate about whether he inherited Bush Sr.'s concerns regarding masculinity, along with his name and his job. We don't know the psychological consequences of having a paternal role model who was publicly humiliated for his perceived effeminacy. We *do* know that Bush Jr. has been preoccupied with rectifying what many fellow conservatives have viewed as Bush Sr.'s greatest failure of manly determi-

nation—leaving Saddam Hussein in power, and worse, doing so at the behest of that decidedly unphallic, collaborative institution, the United Nations.[20]

The two Bushes are not unique: they are only the most visible of those men motivated to embrace right-wing politics not by their masculinity but rather by their fear of losing it.

Boys learn and model such attitudes at an early age. To be labeled a sissy is to endure shame and humiliation and sometimes worse. Boys accordingly learn that cross-gender behavior (like playing with dolls) is a taboo enforced by family, peers, and the larger society. To be nurturing and sensitive, in our society, is to model female-ascribed behaviors; fathers who view being a nurturing and sensitive parent as "too feminine" risk raising sons who are insecure about their manhood and who repeat the cycle of defensive hypermasculinity themselves as adults. "For men to be inoculated against appeals to their gender insecurities, we as a society will need to challenge the notion that masculinity must be based on domination, whether over women or over other men," Ducat concludes. "This will require far more than an intellectual debate, however; nothing short of a thoroughgoing transformation in the way boys grow into men will be needed."[21]

The Masculine Mystique

If American men have worried about being wimpy, then American women have similarly faced their own fears about femininity and what society expects from them. For example, in the late 1950s and early 1960s, some American women began to express unease about their lot in life, about what society expected from them—which, according to more than a few fashion magazines and television shows, seemed to center around cooking and cleaning and greeting their husbands at the door with martinis. As they generally did their best to live up to the ideal defined by Harriet Nelson in the emblematic television show *Ozzie and Harriet*, some wondered whether there should not be more to their existence. Betty Friedan best articulated this distress in her groundbreaking book *The Feminine Mystique* (1963), in which she wrote,

> It was a strange stirring, a sense of dissatisfaction, a yearning that women suffered in the middle of the twentieth century in the United States. Each suburban wife struggled with it alone. As she made the beds, shopped for groceries, matched slipcover material, ate peanut butter sandwiches with her children, chauffeured Cub Scouts and Brownies, lay beside her husband at night—she was afraid to ask even of herself the silent question—"Is this all?"[22]

Friedan aptly captured the "problem with no name": the question of female fulfillment, boxed in by the sometimes limiting qualities deemed central to being an American women.

It seems quite possible that the constellation of masculine qualities admired by Americans marks a kind of masculine mystique, in contrast to the feminine mystique identified by Friedan. Stoicism, reserve, toughness, and forcefulness all hover at the top of the list of qualities that American society seems to admire in its men. These qualities have remained remarkably constant over the course of the nineteenth and twentieth centuries, with some fluctuation in the 1970s, when the masculine mystique came under scrutiny with a reevaluation of traditional gender roles in the aftermath of the women's liberation movement. American men of the 1970s were portrayed as sensitive, New Age guys, in touch with their inner women, but these feminized masculinities were doomed to die, barely outlasting the decade as men fought to hang onto that which they thought made them men. Some cultural signifiers from the early 1980s reveal notions of American manhood in transition. One can read Bruce Feirstein's tongue-in-cheek *Real Men Don't Eat Quiche: A Guidebook to All That Is Truly Masculine* (1982) from cover to cover and still not have a clear understanding of how men are supposed to behave: it is unclear exactly what the author is advocating. For example, he conveys displeasure with the Alan Alda–ization of America, which he argues has created "a nation of wimps," but he does not advocate a return to stereotypical, 1950s-era gender roles. "Unlike his predecessors, today's Real Man actually can feel things like sorrow, pity, love, warmth, and sincerity; but, he'd never be so vulnerable as to admit them," writes Feirstein. Even though today's Real Man does not belong to the National Rifle Association, violence is still a viable option. One can always fall back on the "one simple rule" of the Real Man's timeless credo: "Never settle with words what you can accomplish with a flamethrower."[23]

Perhaps not surprisingly, men in the 1980s sought answers in the newest versions of the Hollywood icons who had defined American masculinity over the course of the century. The popular heroes of the 1980s—Hollywood stars like Sylvester Stallone, Mel Gibson, and Bruce Willis—complemented the decade's biggest action hero, President Ronald Reagan, himself embodying the success, toughness, and strength that made his political ascendancy possible. "Reagan cast himself as a hero," writes Susan Jeffords in *Hard Bodies: Hollywood Masculinity in the Reagan Era* (1994), "but many in the country seemed to be reading from the same script."[24] Hollywood macho men in the 1980s were populist heroes, different from the vigilantes that typified action heroes of the 1970s (such as Clint Eastwood or Charles Bronson); just as Willis's character in the *Die Hard* series stood for the will and desire of the average citizen in defiance of institutional bureaucracy, Reagan too stood against big government. Jeffords asserts, "Ronald Reagan became the premiere masculine archetype for the 1980s, embodying both national and individual images of manliness that came to underlie the nation's identity during his eight years in office."[25] In this way, masculine physicality, individual determination, and a willingness to use violence all defined American national identity as reflected in both politics and popular culture.

Perhaps the earlier insecurities of the 1970s spoke to a paradigm shift in gender construction—a realization by American men that, all told, it does not really mean much of anything to be a man—or a woman, for that matter. Perhaps Americans had begun to realize that we are all just people with different genders and different plumbing and different sexual preferences, and perhaps it is not the differences but the commonalities we share as people that mean something. More likely, the older notions of masculinity never went away: they were simply tempered in the fires of modern feminism. And most important—be it a 1970s-era feminized masculinity, a 1980s-era hypermasculinized masculinity, or a 1990s-era anxiety-ridden masculinity—these masculinities have all moved on a fulcrum of violence, an assumption of male superiority based on threat of force.

Ornamental Culture and the American Male

In the 1990s, feminist scholars proved to be the harshest critics and fiercest allies of American men as they scouted the ever-changing terrain of masculinity; some even proved to be both. For example, when Susan Faludi published her best-selling *Backlash: The Undeclared War against American Women* (1991), she alienated a number of American men who resented her depiction of them as dogged resisters of feminism. In *Stiffed: The Betrayal of the American Man* (1999), she appeased some of those same men by arguing that men had not failed American society so much as their culture had failed them. The problems that beleaguered American men, "buffeted by the collapse of [post–World War II] society's promise," were external—not internal.

In *Stiffed*, an epic journalistic endeavor, Faludi set out not only to listen to American men but also to explain how a media-driven culture changed the rules of what it expects from them. Her journey began at a domestic-violence group in Long Beach, California, where she found "prototypical modern wife beaters, who, demographic research suggests, are commonly ill equipped to fulfill the requirements of expected stereotypical sex roles, men who are socially isolated, afflicted with a sense of ineffectuality, and have nothing but the gender rule book to fall back on." She continued: "The men had probably felt in control when they beat their wives, but their everyday existence was of feeling controlled—a feeling they had no way of expressing because to reveal it was less than masculine, would make each of them, in fact, 'no man at all.' For such men, the desire to be in charge was what they felt they must do to survive in a nation that *expected* them to dominate."[26] Faludi found in these men something representative of American men in general. Her experience with them challenged her assumptions about men in the United States, whom she began to recognize as riddled with their own self-doubts and questions about who they were. Like Stephen Ducat, she found insecurity where she thought she would find bravado and machismo.

While Faludi saw the crisis in American masculinity as one related to control, she explored control not in terms of agency but in terms of *lack* of agency. In this view, masculinity is a matter of motion and action:

> The man controlling his environment is today the prevailing American image of masculinity. A man is expected to prove himself not by being part of society but by being untouched by it, soaring above it. He is to travel unfettered, beyond society's clutches, alone—making or breaking whatever or whoever crosses his path. He is to be in the driver's seat, the king of the road, forever charging down the open highway, along the masculine Möbius strip that cycles endlessly through a numbing stream of movies, TV shows, novels, advertisements, and pop tunes. He's a man because he won't be stopped. He'll fight attempts to tamp him down; if he has to, he'll use his gun. It seems to us as if it has always been thus, ever since the first white frontiersman strode into the New World wilderness, his rifle at the ready.[27]

After convincingly showing that notions of manhood have in fact changed, becoming more individualistic and less communitarian during the twentieth century, she posited, "What gets discussed is how men are exercising or abusing their control and power, not whether a lack of mooring, a lack of context, is causing their anguish."[28]

Faludi identified what she called a new "ornamental culture," changed fundamentally "from a society that produced a culture to a culture rooted in no real world at all." The American culture she described was jewel-like, with millions of facets radiating not outward but inward, reflecting one another. This society confounded traditional gender roles and left much doubt over how to behave and act. "Where we once lived in a society in which men in particular participated by being useful in public life," she wrote, "we now are surrounded by a culture that encourages people to play almost no functional public roles, only decorative or consumer ones." This ornamental culture increased aggression and fed violent behaviors at the end of the twentieth century:

> By the end of the American Century, every outlet of the consumer world—magazines, ads, movies, sports, music videos—would deliver the message that manhood had become a performance game to be won in the marketplace, not the workplace, and that male anger was now part of the show. An ornamental culture encouraged young men to see surliness, hostility, and violence as expressions of glamour, a way to showcase themselves without being feminized before an otherwise potentially girlish mirror.[29]

As a result, American men found themselves surrounded by a dearth of true male friends, an overabundance of women who questioned their manhood, and a host of potential enemies. "At the close of the century, men find themselves in an unfamiliar world where male worth is measured only by participation in a celebrity-driven consumer culture and awarded by lady luck."[30]

Falling Down

If Faludi was correct, then American men have, inevitably and unavoidably, acted out culturally prescribed images of manhood. Different writers have identified these archetypes: Leonard Glass's "Man's Man" and "Ladies' Man," Leslie Fiedler's "Good Bad Boy," Faludi's own "Bad Bad Boy."[31] Different public figures—be they John Wayne, Arnold Schwarzenegger, Tupac Shakur, or George W. Bush—embody the admirable traits of any given moment in American time, and these traits seem to form a fairly consistent constellation of qualities (power, strength, and individualism, for example). More often than not, the brightest stars in this constellation are assertiveness, aggression, and a willingness to employ violence to achieve a given objective. Faludi explained this phenomenon historically: "As the male role has diminished amid a sea of betrayed promises, many men have found themselves driven to more domineering and some even 'monstrous' displays in their frantic quest for a meaningful showdown."[32]

One film that explored such monstrous displays triggered a media avalanche of stories about middle-class white rage when it was released. With the tagline "The adventures of an ordinary man at war with the everyday world," *Falling Down* (1993) starred Michael Douglas as an out-of-work defense contractor who experiences a postmodern meltdown in Los Angeles; an unfortunate series of events combine to overwhelm the protagonist who, overwrought and overwhelmed, reacts violently. The *New Yorker* described the film as a "crude vigilante picture disguised as social satire," with the reviewer wryly noting, "It's no small feat to turn a sociopath into a martyr, but the director, Joel Schumacher, and the screenwriter, Ebbe Roe Smith, are up to the challenge."[33] Other reviews smiled more favorably on the film. Film critic Roger Ebert, for example, wrote,

> What is fascinating about the Douglas character, as written and played, is the core of sadness in his soul. Yes, by the time we meet him, he has gone over the edge. But there is no exhilaration in his rampage, no release. He seems weary and confused, and in his actions he unconsciously follows scripts that he may have learned from the movies, or on the news, where other frustrated misfits vent their rage on innocent bystanders.[34]

This notion of a character portraying a real person following a script to order his life resonates with Faludi's notion of the ubiquity of culturally prescribed images of manhood. The simulacrum of American masculinity self-refers endlessly, like a mirror held in front of another mirror.

Such monstrous displays seemed to peak in the mid-1990s, when school shootings, drive-bys, and employees "going postal" at the workplace dominated headlines. Perhaps no other single event dramatized this crazed sense of a world gone mad better than Shawn Nelson's 1995 tank rampage in San Diego. Nelson was a thirty-five-year-old plumber and Army veteran living in southern California. Divorced, hospitalized for painful back and neck injuries, and depressed, Nelson's problems multiplied exponentially when he turned to drugs for relief in 1993. Losing not only his livelihood to robbers (who stole his valuable work equipment) but also his parents to cancer, Nelson contemplated suicide, but instead climbed into his Chevy van at dusk on May 17, 1995, and drove to the National Guard Armory in Kearny Mesa, California, where he—in what can only be described as an astounding lapse in security—hijacked a fifty-seven-ton M-60 Patton tank. Nelson led police on a twenty-three-minute, forty-five-mile-per-hour chase through suburban San Diego, where he crushed everything in his path before wedging the vehicle on a concrete highway divider. He was shot to death by police, who accessed the tank's interior using bolt cutters. Interestingly, this real-life event was preceded by a film with an eerily similar plot: *Tank*, a 1984 potboiler starring James Garner and C. Thomas Howell, features a career military man who commandeers a vintage Sherman tank to exact justice on an evil southern sheriff.[35]

Invariably, males were at the epicenters of these cultural earthquakes, from Oklahoma City to Columbine. Boys and men pushed to their breaking points seemed to find manhood in such flashpoints. The most monstrous of displays occurred on April 20, 1999, at Columbine High School in Littleton, Colorado. "Everyone with a white cap or baseball cap, stand up!" Eric Harris and Dylan Klebold allegedly said before their shooting rampage in the school library. "All jocks stand up! We'll get the guys in white hats!" After Columbine, a number of critics pointed to the easy availability of guns and the shooters' obsession with violent video games. Few, however, discussed the deep-seated fear underlying much school violence: being perceived as a sissy. Klebold and Harris did what they did to assert their own sense of selves, to flex their egos and prove their manhood to those who mattered most—the peers who rejected them and valued them least—and they sought to do so in a highly public way.[36]

From Rape Culture to Girl Nation

Where is American masculinity now? In July 2006, *Esquire* magazine devoted an entire issue to "The State of the American Man," and found that boys, in particular, are in a state of disarray. Culling statistics from a variety of sources—including the U.S. Census Bureau, the Centers for Disease Control and Prevention (CDC), the National Institute of Health, the National Center for Education Statistics, and the Department of Justice—*Esquire* painted a troubling portrait of American boyhood in crisis. It found that boys are more likely to score worse on standardized reading and writing tests, more likely to be held back in school, more likely to drop out of school. If they do graduate from high school, they are less likely to go to college; if they do go to college, they are less likely to graduate and more likely to get lower grades. Boys are twice as likely to be diagnosed with an attention-deficit or learning disorder, and twice as likely to abuse alcohol. Certain statistics are particularly telling in their lopsidedness. Boys are five times as likely to kill themselves and sixteen times as likely to go to prison; 95 percent of state and federal prisoners under the age of twenty-five are male.[37]

Evidence shows that this crisis in American boyhood has been going on for at least the past two decades. In the years before Columbine, groups of young men had marauded fellow citizens in incidents tagged by journalists as "wilding," or indulging destructive impulses without regard for consequence. "To white middle-class Americans, wilding symbolized something real and terrifying about life in the United States at the turn of the decade," writes Charles Derber in his book *The Wilding of America* (1996). "Things were falling apart, at least in the hearts of America's major cities."[38] One event in particular demonstrated this collapse of civility. On the evening of April 19, 1989, a young woman, out for a jog through New York's Central Park, was bludgeoned, raped, sodomized, and beaten so savagely that doctors feared for her life; she was left for dead in the park by approximately forty teenage boys who later laughed about the incident when apprehended. The assault on the Central Park jogger marked the first of the monstrous displays that came to define the following decade; writers at the *New York Post* and other newspapers coined the term "wilding" to describe the event. For years, the public did not know the name of the twenty-eight-year-old Ivy League graduate who had been beaten within a breath of her life; Trisha Meili revealed her own identity in 2003.[39]

The Meili attack was an extreme and highly publicized example of the kind of violence that occurs in the United States everyday. The masculine mystique surely accommodates a certain level of violence directed toward women; if we interpret masculinity to include an expectation of violence, then it seems unavoidable that such violence would affect relations between the sexes. Here in the United States, statistics tell an ugly tale of male violence directed toward the women they supposedly love. For example, the FBI reports that one-third of female murder victims in the United States are killed by their male domestic partners. More women are injured by domestic violence than by muggings, stranger rape, and car accidents *combined*. According to the American Medical Association, one-third of women's emergency-room visits are attributable to spousal abuse.[40] Violence may be considered a male problem insofar as men perpetrate violence far more than women; however, this characterization, while accurately describing the source of violence, hardly suffices to describe its outcome. It has been women, not men, who have not only endured patriarchal domination for thousands of years but also suffered violence disproportionately at the hands of men.

Some scholars have even suggested that we live in a rape culture, insofar as rape continues to be a pervasive fact of American life.[41] Surely the statistics on sex crime suggest as much, and if the underlying attitudes expressed in our society are any indicator, then this characterization may not be far from the truth. It is not only stranger rape but also a host of other sexual crimes, including date rape and spousal abuse, that compose this culture, creating an environment in which men can justify their sexual aggression; when one considers pornography (especially in electronic media) and sexual harassment (in schools and workplaces), the contours of a rape culture become even clearer. The entitlement men feel toward women's bodies is only exacerbated by the depiction of women as sexual prey in popular fashion magazines, on billboards, and on television.

If violence is largely a male phenomenon, then women are increasingly modeling male behaviors of violence; girls, in particular, seem more comfortable in "acting like boys" in this regard. From exclusion and social isolation in the 1980s to bullying in the early 1990s and physical violence in the late 1990s, aggression by girls seemed to be rising; today, girls account for 28 percent of the juvenile arrests for violent crime, according to a recent study. More girls are entering the juvenile justice system because they have committed a violent crime, and they are doing so at younger ages.[42] Deborah Prothrow-Stith and Howard R. Spivak, authors of *Sugar and Spice and No Longer Nice* (2005), have explained this trend as a kind of logical evolution of the women's movement: as girls enter traditionally male spheres, they are increasingly socialized in the same ways as boys, and as they are exposed to some of the same violent images, role models, and social expectations as boys, they are now responding with more aggressive and violent behavior. They are learning to be violent, just as boys have done over the centuries.

Girl violence is certainly not as widespread as boy violence. Violence has been and remains a predominantly male behavior; but the transgendered growth of this kind of outward expression of anger, more typical of boys and men, represents a troubling new problem. Violence threatens to become a normative pattern of behavior for any young American, regardless of gender. What can be done to arrest this trend before it pervades social relations across the board? It seems clear that boys and men should be models for neither handling anger nor resolving conflicts; in copying boys in this regard, girls model the worst of male behaviors. The answer lies, perhaps, not in hardening women but in softening men—that is, in socializing boys to be less like louts.

CHAPTER 2

Televiolence

When television is good, nothing—not the
theater, not the magazines or newspapers—is
better. But when television is bad, nothing is
worse. I invite you to sit down in front of your
television set when your station goes on the air
and . . . keep your eyes glued to that set until
the station signs off. I can assure you that you
will observe a vast wasteland. You will see a
procession of game shows, violence, audience
participation shows, formula comedies about
unbelievable families, blood and thunder,
mayhem, violence, sadism, murder, western
bad men, western good men, private eyes,
gangsters, more violence, and cartoons.
—Newton Minow, chairman of the Federal
Communications Commission (FCC), 1961

In 1961 I worried that my children would not
benefit much from television, but in 1991, I
worry that my grandchildren will actually be
harmed by it.
—Newton Minow, 1991

Research, Policy, and Public Concern

In 1954, Senator Estes Kefauver, chairman of the Senate Sub-
committee on Juvenile Delinquency, held hearings on whether
television violence was contributing to real-life violence in the
United States. When queried, network executives pled ignorance, claiming that the available research was not conclusive.

We just do not know, they said; there is not enough evidence. As the first generation of TV watchers matured, parents and teachers were left to fall back on common sense, which suggested that watching a lot of violence could hurt a person, spiritually and mentally. The psyches of children seemed particularly susceptible because it was clearly harder for them to discern virtual violence from the real thing. The entertainment industry, however, assured the viewing public that watching violence caused no ill effects. Because there was no outcry in favor of limiting violent media representations (which, after all, many people seemed to like and enjoy), television programmers were able to continue business as usual over the second half of the twentieth century, as levels of TV violence steadily increased alongside levels of real-life violence.

If broadcasters could once plausibly deny a link between media violence and real-world violence, then surely the average citizen can no longer profess ignorance with regard to the possible harms of watching violent media. The half-century of research on television violence has resulted in a wide range of surveys and experiments, most of which confirm the suspicion that viewing violence can be harmful, and in recent years public awareness of the dangers of viewing violence has caught up to what researchers already know, and to what media moguls have traditionally failed to acknowledge. "A clear and consistent pattern of empirical results has emerged from over four decades of research on the effects of media violence," writes one leading expert.

> Media violence is a contributor to aggressive behavior in the short run and, for children, at least, to aggressive behavior in the long run and even into adulthood. It is not the only factor accounting for individual differences in aggressiveness, nor even the most important factor. But as the mix of laboratory experiments, field experiments, cross-sectional survey studies, longitudinal survey studies, and meta-analyses show, it is a significant factor.[1]

In 1972, the surgeon general's report *Television and Growing Up: The Impact of Televised Violence* provided an authoritative warning, as did the National Institute of Mental Health in 1982 and the American Psychological Association in 1992; health care providers have since agreed on the dangers. On July 26, 2000, the American Medical Association, the American Academy of Pediatrics, the American Psychiatric Association, the American Psychological Association, the American Academy of Family Physicians, and the American Academy of Child and Adolescent Psychiatry issued a "Joint Statement on the Impact of Entertainment Violence on Children." An excerpt of the statement, which was subsequently endorsed by both houses of the U.S. Congress, reads, "The conclusion of the public health community, based on over 30 years of research, is that viewing entertainment violence can lead to increases in aggressive attitudes, values and behavior, particularly in children."[2]

In addressing whether or not media violence causes real-life violence, skeptics have been quick to observe that some studies on the effects of media violence have been flawed, and that correlation does not prove causation. Millions of people view televised violence every day without subsequently acting in an overtly violent fashion, they correctly point out, and the many studies that have sought to prove or disprove a causal link certainly warrant a degree of skepticism. There is some evidence that media violence "makes people more violent"—that is, that it directly translates into post-viewing, violent behavior—but the evidence is largely anecdotal and limited to certain individuals. Few knowledgeable individuals would argue that a sustained causal relationship has been proven between media violence and violence in society.

But, as Newton Minow, professor of communications law and policy at Northwestern University and former chairman of the Federal Communications Commission (FCC)—has observed, "Social science is not in the proof business, but in the business of identifying relationships and measuring their significance, strength, and direction," and the relationships between media violence and so-called real-life violence are measurably strong and undeniably significant.[3] For those won over by empirical studies demonstrating causality, there is lots of research showing that prolonged viewing of violent imagery can increase aggression toward others, desensitize viewers to real-life violence, and increase fear of becoming a victim of violence. Such were the findings of the 1994 National Television Violence Study, a three-year effort by researchers from four universities, overseen by several national policy organizations; others have confirmed these findings. There is also evidence that prolonged viewing of violent imagery can cause disinhibition—that is, the viewing of violent media can remove or reduce reservations that people may have with regard to performing aggressive acts that they already know. In theory, seeing Bugs Bunny blow up Wile E. Coyote with a case of Acme dynamite, or seeing Arnold Schwarzenegger machine-gun his way through waves of nameless enemy soldiers, can disinhibit unrelated acts of aggression (such as pushing, shoving, and hitting) in viewers.[4] Future studies may confirm disinhibition as one of the more onerous and dangerous effects of watching violent imagery.

Informed by more and newer research findings, the responses of policy makers have followed the ebb and flow of public concern in the aftermath of multiple shootings and national tragedies, and certain politicians have led attempts to stir interest and even to initiate regulation; however, these attempts have historically folded to industry promises of self-policing. Much like the Motion Picture Association of America (MPAA) rating system established in 1967 that grades films based on content, the Entertainment Software Ratings Board rating system established in 1994 labels video games with age-appropriate warnings and guidelines. In 2000, the Federal Trade Commission (FTC) issued a report on the marketing of violent movies, music, and video games to children in which it recommended improvement in all three related industries. At that time, the film industry narrowly avoided federal regulation of its advertising practices as politicians, in the wake of the Columbine High School shootings, called studio executives before a congressional investigative committee; as the government has done in the past, the committee eventually allowed Hollywood to police itself. In 2004, thirty-nine members of the U.S. House of Representatives asked the FCC to undertake an inquiry on television violence; that same year, the FTC reported that in its tests of the MPAA rating system, 36 percent of underage buyers were able to purchase tickets for R-rated movies without an age check; it also reported that 81 percent of underage buyers were able to buy R-rated DVDs without an age verification. In 2005, the unlikely team of Senators Joseph Lieberman, Sam Brownback, Hillary Rodham Clinton, and Rick Santorum introduced a bill that called for $90 million to fund studies on media effects.[5]

Since the 1999 Columbine massacre sparked an outcry over games and violence, lawmakers in several states have proposed bans on the sale of violent video games. For example, Representative Joe Baca, D-California, introduced bills in the U.S. House of Representatives in 2002 and 2003 that would have made it a misdemeanor to sell or rent violent or sexually graphic games to minors, and Rod Blagojevich, governor of Illinois, signed a similar law in 2005. However, no bill that has become law has survived legal challenges based on First Amendment protection. The video game industry, much like the film industry, has successfully argued that the government cannot restrict the sale of nonobscene games, just as it cannot impose restrictions on books or music.[6]

Responding to public concern and political pressure, the FCC released its much-anticipated report on violent television programming on April 25, 2007. For the first time, the federal government hinted at the possibility of forthcoming regulation. "We recognize that violent content is a protected form of speech under the First Amendment, but note that the government interests at stake, such as protecting children from excessively violent television programming, are similar to those which have been found to justify other content-based regulations," the agency stated. "We find that although the V-chip and TV ratings system appear useful in the abstract, they are not effective at protecting children from violent content for a number of reasons. In particular, we find that the TV ratings system has certain weaknesses that prevent parents from screening out much programming that they find objectionable." In issuing its report, the FCC seemed to agree with Governor Blagojevich, who had stated in 2005, "Parents don't need the government to raise their kids. That's their job. But government can help them protect their children from influences they may not want their kids exposed to."[7]

Looking for Keys

Just as a handful of scientists claim that cigarettes do not cause cancer, a handful of researchers claim that media violence has no ill effects on viewers, and some of them have made rather forceful arguments. Jonathan Freedman, a psychologist at the University of Toronto and author of *Media Violence and Its Effects on Aggression: Assessing the Scientific Evidence* (2002), has delved into some of the more than two hundred studies that directly assess the effects of exposure to media violence on aggression and desensitization. He has found that scientific research has *not* proven that media violence causes children or adults to become more aggressive or commit violent crimes. Far fewer than half of the psychological and sociological studies done in this area have found a causal connection, according to Freedman—in fact, the research could be interpreted as showing that there is *no* causal effect of media violence at all. Some within the entertainment industry have touted the book as evidence that media violence has no ill effects on children.

Freedman's meta-analysis certainly raises doubts about the validity of some earlier studies; however, its greatest accomplishment may be the way it exposes the limits of psychological studies in studying aggression. Freedman effectively pokes holes in every single study he revisits: this study is flawed for this reason, that study is flawed for that reason. *None* of the studies he examines effectively measures the causal relation between media violence and real-world violence. The ideal way to test the effects of media violence on aggressive behavior would be a long-term study in a natural setting with all other variables isolated and accounted for; however, Freedman acknowledges that such a lab or field experiment would be impossible. "I think most people's main concern about media violence is that it has effects that show up when our children have grown up," he writes. "Laboratory research cannot address this concern. Field experiments are also quite limited in this respect, but they are much better than laboratory experiments." He rather glumly notes, "The most we can conclude is that there probably is a relationship, but scientific evidence for it is quite limited."[8]

Media Violence and Its Effects on Aggression might have effectively ended the debate surrounding the ill effects of media violence were it not for two problems. The first relates to the objectivity of the study. In the preface, Freedman raises a red flag when he writes, "In 1999 I was approached by the Motion Picture Association of America and asked whether I would consider conducting a comprehensive review of all the research on media violence. Until then I had never received any support from any organization for this work. . . . I was a little nervous because I knew that there was a danger that my work would be tainted by a connection with the MPAA." It is an honest but damning admission on Freedman's part. The author reveals that, after some hand-wringing, he decided to undertake the MPAA-commissioned study; he does not reveal the extent to which the MPAA, Hollywood's leading lobbying group, underwrote his study. "Although I was nervous about being tainted," Freedman writes, "I am confident that I was not."[9]

The author assures the reader that he maintained his academic integrity in doing this research, and the reader must rely on trust, knowing that the MPAA has consistently defended the rights of screenwriters and directors to depict any manner of things on the big screen—including graphically violent scenes—in the name of First Amendment expression. Of course, if a researcher were approached by the National Rifle Association to study the impact of gun availability on school shootings, then one would have to consider the findings with a certain degree of skepticism—particularly if that researcher determined that decades of countervailing scholarship was wrong and that, in fact, there was no causal relation between guns and school shootings.

While the first problem revolves around bias, the second revolves around methodology. The key question of the book is whether or not media violence causes aggression in viewers. Freedman sets out to conduct an exhaustive review of the existing scholarship on media violence and its effects on aggressive tendencies. "Having looked at all this research," he writes, "I concluded that the results do not support the view that exposure to media violence causes children or anyone else to become aggressive or to commit crimes; nor does it support the idea that it causes people to be less sensitive to real violence."[10]

His evaluation of the studies may be sound, but what of the original experiments? According to one observer, a psychologist studying what has been studied before is "like the drunk looking for a lost set of keys under a lamppost because the light is better there."[11] In other words, in looking for a causal relationship between media violence and real-world violence, a scholar risks adopting the same fallacious assumptions that led his predecessors down a path toward erroneous conclusions.

A better starting point might be to ask: In what ways, if any, does media violence enable actual violence? Why? The search for direct causal relations in proximal and distal sources of media influence yields limited results; in Freedman's case, as in the experiments he studies, it yields yes-or-no answers that only partially illuminate the issue. As Douglas Gentile and Arturo Sesma Jr. have observed, to the extent that we expect media effects to be exhibited in an obvious manner, we are missing opportunities to see other less obvious and perhaps more pervasive effects.[12]

A fair answer to the question "Does media violence cause real-life violence?" would be "sometimes" or "often not directly," but this overly simplistic question misses much of the subtlety of how people interpret and act upon what they see. "When we ask about the effects of the mass media [on children], we must not phrase the question in terms of *whether* the media have an effect," notes Eleanor Maccoby, "but rather *how much* effect on *what kind* of children, and under *what circumstances* will the effects be exhibited."[13] The effects of media are usually neither simple nor direct, and most often occur at a level below conscious awareness; advertisers who attempt to sway consumer-buying habits know this fact well. "Most media effects are cumulative and subtle, even when they are designed to influence behavior," write Gentile and Sesma. "This subtlety masks remarkable power and persuasiveness."[14]

Imitation and Copycat Violence

Of course, sometimes these effects are neither cumulative nor subtle, as when on-screen violence translates directly into real-world violence; in such instances, claims that media violence has no ill effects tend to ring hollow. Whether violent movies inspire certain individuals to act violently, or whether violent individuals are drawn to particular films or television shows because of the violence depicted therein, the net outcome is the same: the power of film and the pervasiveness of television augment the effects of on-screen violence. Like adults, children often imitate what they see on TV; the difference is that children more often do it deliberately. Able to convince themselves that they are beyond media effects, adults more often imitate what they see unconsciously or subconsciously; however, adults too style their lives based on the televised fictions of Hollywood and of the advertising world, and some even model on-screen violence. Wannabe thugs copy what they learn from gangster movies; in fact, Hollywood created the Hays Code, the often maligned 1934 production code that dictated what could and could not be depicted on-screen, not only to stave off censorship but also to deflect charges that it was spreading gangsterism. Newspapers frequently carry stories that suggest that violent offenders model their behavior on what they view on-screen, and such incidents have been well documented since the inception of film and television.[15]

Such violence is often exacerbated by extensive media coverage. Loren Coleman has discussed this tendency in *The Copycat Effect: How the Media and Popular Culture Trigger the Mayhem in Tomorrow's Headlines* (2004), in which he describes what he calls the "dirty little secret" of mass media. "The media's graphic coverage of rampage shootings, celebrity suicides, bridge jumpers, school shootings, and the like is triggering vulnerable and angry people to take their own lives and that of others," Coleman argues. "Their use of the phrase ['copycat phenomenon'] seems to put a distance between the events and the reporting media, and allows them the stance that implies *they are not part of the problem*," he writes. "But they are."[16]

Movies have inspired their share of carnage, according to Coleman. Stanley Kubrick's film *A Clockwork Orange* was linked to so many copycat crimes in the early 1970s that Kubrick himself had the film taken out of circulation. By 1986, psychiatrists Alan Berman and Thomas Radecki had documented forty-three deaths worldwide since the 1978 release of *The Deer Hunter* that could be attributed to imitations of that film's Russian-roulette scenes. In the mid-1990s, Oliver Stone's *Natural Born Killers* inspired killing sprees by loners and star-crossed lovers alike.[17]

Coleman describes how mass shooters and serial killers often learn from one another, participating in a deadly game of one-upmanship. For example, on October 16, 1991, George Hennard crashed his 1987 Ford Ranger pickup truck into Luby's Cafeteria in Killeen, Texas, and sprayed it with gunfire, killing twenty-two people with a Glock 17 and a Ruger P89 (two 9mm pistols) before killing himself with a shot to his head. It was probably no coincidence that Hennard, before committing the worst mass murder in U.S. history (up to that point), had watched a video documentary at his house about James Huberty, who had killed *twenty-one* people at a McDonald's in California on July 18, 1984. Coleman also describes how the nation's schools endured a barrage of copycat threats in the wake of the Columbine shootings; he notes that some four hundred related incidents were reported in the month following the killings in Littleton. Coleman, an expert on suicide clusters, also describes how rock star Kurt Cobain, who killed himself in 1994, apparently inspired many young fans to follow suit. When the online Nirvana Fan Club reported the death of a fourteen-year-old Italian girl, the webmaster observed, "This is the 68th copycat suicide I have heard about."[18]

With regard to violence in a media-saturated age, there is no such thing as a localized problem. If a celebrity suicide is widely reported, for example, the suicide rate will rise in the following month, according to the copycat effect. In the wake of reports of anthrax-laced letters sent to the American Media Inc. building in Boca Raton, Florida, other mail-borne "attacks" followed in the fall of 2001, when American fears of biological warfare peaked in the wake of the destruction of the World Trade Center. Some were perhaps genuine, most were harmless white powders meant to look like anthrax, but all were copycat incidents. Coleman does not argue that the media should stop reporting the news—only that journalists should practice responsible journalism. He pleas for the mass media to stop sensationalizing shootings and suicides "the way it uses tornadoes, hurricanes, and earthquakes to get people to watch their programs." To run a story on suicide or gangland murder without thinking about the collateral damage the story might cause is "like giving a child a loaded gun," he concludes.[19]

On-screen violence sometimes inspires the real thing, but seldom are the effects of the mass media so stark. Memetics, or the study of memes as contagious ideas, passing from person to person much like a virus, offers some insight into thought contagion and the infectious evolution of cultural transference; however, most scholars—like Freedman and the scholars he studies—have focused upon direct connections between media violence and "real-life" violence, and it is here that research has failed to illuminate fully the subtleties of how we are affected by what we see.

The Positives of Viewing Violence

In addition to those who claim that viewing violence has no negative effects, others have pushed counterarguments even further, arguing that viewing violence can have *positive* effects. In his persuasive homage to popular culture, *Killing Monsters: Why Children Need Fantasy, Super Heroes, and Make-Believe Violence* (2002), Gerard Jones explains why children need violence in their lives. Kids adore violent entertainment not because they have been brainwashed by the media, he argues, but because it gives them coping skills they want and need. "I've seen young people turn every form of imaginary aggression into sources of emotional nourishment and developmental support," he assures.

> It is easy to fall into the trap of thinking that young people
> emulate literally what they see in entertainment. That
> if they like a rapper who insults gays, then they must be
> learning hostility to gays, and if they love a movie hero who
> defeats villainy with a gun, then they must be learning to
> solve problems with violence. There is some truth in that.
> One of the functions of stories and games is to help children
> rehearse for what they'll be in later life. Anthropologists and
> psychologists who study play, however, have shown that there
> are many other functions as well—one of which is to enable

children to pretend to be just what they know they'll *never* be. Exploring, in a safe and controlled context, what is impossible or too dangerous or forbidden to them is a crucial tool in accepting the limits of reality. Playing with rage is a valuable way to reduce its power. Being evil and destructive in imagination is a vital compensation for the wildness we all have to surrender on our way to being good people.[20]

In this view, role-playing Darth Vader and hacking away at Jedi knights with an imaginary light saber would therefore signal healthy role-playing, not aberrant behavior.

Fantasy violence is important in helping kids validate certain feelings, trust their own emotions, and process information, according to Jones; to him, aggression is not necessarily a bad thing. "What if most of them [aggressive children] are channeling that aggression into self-assertion, healthy competition, increased energy, determination, and courage?" he asks. "By failing to consider the *meaning* of children's behaviors, we do worse than render the research useless. We risk reading it upside down, seeing only negatives where we should be seeing positives, and so taking tools from children that may be helping them deal with the very stresses that concern us."[21] From Jones's perspective, toy guns are not stand-ins used symbolically to replicate weapons, but rather wands, used magically to defeat the formidable foes of children's imaginations. Roughhousing dissipates fear; mock combat helps kids learn how to judge dangers and take appropriate risks. "I believe we burden children with something they shouldn't have to carry when we dump our adult anxieties inappropriately on their fantasies," he writes.[22]

Like Jones, scholars such as Maria Tatar have explained the socializing effect of children's fairy tales in expressing the forbidden, modulating fear by caricaturing reality, and providing an opportunity for parental guidance. The pedagogy of fear not only scares children into proper behaviors but also reaffirms adult notions of right and wrong. Violence recurs in literature and theater because it teaches certain lessons about transgression, poetic justice, and righteous retribution. There is something primordial and archaic about this sort of dramatic violence, according to Dolf Zillmann in his own explanation of Jungian archetypes and the psychological appeal of slaughter.[23]

Jones's argument—an update of Bruno Bettelheim's influential study of fairy tales, *The Uses of Enchantment* (1976)—appeals for a number of reasons. First, it reaffirms the value of play. Second, it soothes and reassures adults, worried about their children turning into little monsters. It encourages parents to lighten up. The oversized toy guns and plastic swords, the faux wrestling in the backyard, and the frenetic video games all seem a bit less ominous when filtered through his schema. Third, it posits that violence might actually serve a healthy purpose. Fourth, and finally, it holds within it the comforting suggestion that nothing need change. Jones's argument, however, should not be read as a tacit approval of all that popular culture has to offer—particularly with regard to children. A subtle warning suffuses the book: entertainment violence must be "cartoony, intense, and unreal" in order for developing brains to process it safely. "What children seek in images of entertainment isn't desensitization to real suffering but images of violence rendered safe and unreal," he cautions.[24]

Dungeons and Dragons Redux

It is exactly that murky interplay between fantasy and reality that has produced the most anxiety about entertainment violence, particularly as it affects children. Parental fears remain fairly constant, even as the sources of those fears change. For example, much like their parents had worried in the 1950s about the dangers of reading comic books, baby boomers in the 1980s worried about their children playing the fantasy role-playing game Dungeons and Dragons (D&D). The dangers for players lurked in subterranean labyrinths; some parents, however, perceived dangers in the limitless scope of the game, in the totally immersive quality of its game play, and in its occult overtones. Countless articles, a film, and a book all helped not only to popularize the game but also to sensationalize it. Most if not all of the fears about the game proved to be for naught, but the controversy surrounding D&D in the 1980s paralleled the controversy surrounding video games a decade later. Was it too violent? Would the fantastical world of D&D bleed into the real world of players? Could young players distinguish between fantasy and reality?

The *Globe and Mail*, a Canadian newspaper, first wrote about the game in 1978, five years after its creation by Gary Gygax, a shoe repairman and game enthusiast from Wisconsin. Gygax mixed medieval legend and lore with the fantasy literature of authors such as J. R. R. Tolkien, Fritz Leiber, and Robert E. Howard to create a unique game that was "too complicated to become a popular family favorite," according to the article. "Dungeons and Dragons is a monstrosity compared to the geometric elegance of backgammon and chess," the article continued. "No board is used. There is seldom a clear-cut winner. The only equipment required is a pencil, paper, and several oddly shaped dice." Unlike board games, D&D depended heavily on the imagination of those who played it: players created characters such as fighters, magic-users, and thieves who relied on swords, spells, and subterfuge to battle mythical monsters and gain treasure. Gygax tried to sell the game to various large companies before it was first marketed in 1974 by TSR Hobbies, which in 1978 estimated there were "no more than 150,000 serious players in the world." While small in number, players were enthusiastic. "The game inspires the sort of fanatic devotion usually associated with mind-bending religious cults," reported the article.[25]

The game first caught on at college campuses, but it eventually snared some post-college adults before filtering down to teenagers and preteens. Each month in 1978, TSR produced four thousand sets of the basic game alone, plus nearly ten thousand supplementary booklets ("modules") for a yearly gross of over $1 million. One year later, TSR was grossing twice that figure, with 300,000 players in the United States and another 100,000 worldwide. The disappearance of a Michigan State University student who played D&D focused national attention on the game around the same time. That Dallas Egbert was sixteen years old with a genius-level IQ only piqued interest in his disappearance on August 15, 1979. Reports surfaced that fantasy role-players at Cal Tech and MSU played a modified, live-action version of D&D in subcampus steam tunnels.

People wondered whether Dallas, losing his grip on reality in a D&D-induced delirium, had vanished into the tunnels. "His disappearance," reported *Newsweek*, "added to the exotic reputation of D&D." A high-profile private investigator flew in from Texas to find Dallas, who turned up one month later, after the investigator found evidence of Dallas's passage through the tunnels below MSU. "Some D&D zealots carry the game to extremes," said *Newsweek*. "But most players understand it's just a game." Sadly, Dallas's problems were much bigger than the twists and turns of any game. He continued to suffer from depression after his reappearance; on August 11, 1980, he committed suicide.[26]

The strange story of Dallas Egbert did not deter people from playing; if anything, it drew more players into the game. Interest in Dungeons and Dragons continued to grow in the following decade. Some high schools began to use it in programs for gifted students. By February 1981, TSR was selling 34,000 D&D starter sets each month, but controversy accompanied success. "Concern about the game arises because the role the player may take could necessitate assuming an evil persona," reported Mary Austin in the *Christian Science Monitor*. "Mistrust stems from the fact that in such a role a player is asked to exploit evil motives to acquire points." The "sustained contemplation of evil" as "a legitimate strategy subordinate only to the higher goal of winning" troubled Austin, whose word choice ("points" and "winning") reflected someone unfamiliar with some of the noncompetitive aspects of the game. To her credit, the reporter tried to present all of the positive aspects of the game (for example, its educational possibilities and its emphasis on imagination and cooperation) as well as its negative aspects (for example, its expense, its addictive quality, and its violence). Her article, one of the better journalistic forays into D&D, provided a fair, balanced critique of the game.[27] That same month, a reporter for the *Washington Post* visited nine- to eleven-year-old gamers at an after-school program at Janney Elementary School in the nation's capital. Most of them wanted to play as fighters, and most of them chose neutral character alignments. "I think neutral's best 'cause you can switch, you can do everything," said one ten-year-old.[28]

A truly terrible made-for-TV film, *Mazes and Monsters*

(1982), further sensationalized D&D. Premiering on CBS, the film starred a young Tom Hanks as a college-age adventurer who, vis-à-vis Dallas Egbert, loses his mind while playing a fantasy role-playing game before disappearing. Based on a novel by Rona Jaffe, *Mazes and Monsters* suggested that those who played D&D did so at their own peril. By the following year, those professionals who once relished the game had begun to view it as a guilty pleasure; a thirty-two-year-old attorney who played the game refused to give his name for a 1983 *Washington Post* article, saying, "When some people hear that you play D&D, they think you're crazy, and I'd rather not give them ammunition."[29] A D.C.-area toy-shop owner discussed misperceptions of the game:

> The game is misunderstood for perhaps two reasons. Most parents don't understand why these kids have their head in a book and aren't outside playing baseball. They're doing it because the daily world is too humdrum and, in the game, they can act out the roles of characters they'd like to be. And then there are some born-again Christian groups which have pointed out that, in D&D, magic works and players can call upon demons to aid them.[30]

One player tried to allay such fears by pointing out that most players chose not to play evil characters. He also noted that "99 percent of the time good triumphs over evil." The article was the first to identify the game's aficionados as nerdy kids; the players at the shop "all seem to be cut from the same brainy high school cloth," the author observed. "No quarterbacks here."[31]

Advocates of D&D found a plethora of advantages to playing the game. First, it lured children away from the television set. The idea was that no matter how bad D&D may have been (and its defenders insisted it was not bad at all), it was still better than television, which turned kids into overweight, passive couch potatoes. James Ward, a TSR executive, emphasized that young people who played D&D were "not being spoon-fed their entertainment." Second, D&D was reading-based, structured around detailed manuals that encouraged research and learning. One toy salesman described the game as an educational experience; indeed, some teachers, particularly educators who worked with gifted students, began to incorporate the game into the classroom, where it required more imaginative participation than traditional lesson plans. A Boston-area camp director gushed, "It is wonderful—it takes children to the outer limits of their imaginations. It's very challenging." Third, playing D&D—contrary to Dear's portrayal in *The Dungeon Master*—was a social activity, involving interaction and cooperation. The amount of time spent preparing and playing, and the continuous nature of the game, which could go on for hours and sometimes even days, encouraged close friendships and camaraderie. While D&D's creator, Gary Gygax, did not mention the cross-gender appeal of the game—perhaps because more males played than females—he did emphasize the game's appeal to all ages; because both adults and children could play, he noted, "there's no generation gap." Of course, the game's biggest appeal was that it was fun. As the introduction to the *Advanced D&D Dungeon Master's Guide* (1979) stated, "D&D is first and foremost a game for the fun and enjoyment of those who seek to use imagination and creativity." [32]

By 1983, TSR had sold 6.5 million D&D game sets, making D&D "one of the top-selling games in the country," with an estimated three to four million players, according to the *Washington Post*. One of those players, a sixteen-year-old in Hanover County, Virginia, shot himself, allegedly after playing D&D at a local high school; investigators found D&D modules in Irving Lee ("Bink") Pulling's room, along with a cryptic suicide note. Pulling's parents, charging that the boy's suicide resulted from playing the game, filed a $1 million lawsuit against the school. In August 1983, the local school board in Arlington, Virginia, "reacting to complaints from parents and recent reports linking the game with bizarre incidents and deaths involving youngsters," banned the game.[33] Reacting to the negative press, TSR began to include a warning against identifying too heavily with characters in its games. A judge dismissed the Pullings' lawsuit in late October, but by then the tales of teenage suicides and cultism had began to resemble the stuff of urban legend.[34]

In 1984, William Dear, the flashy private investigator who

found Dallas Egbert, published his account of the case, *The Dungeon Master: The Disappearance of James Dallas Egbert III*. The suspenseful book paints a fairly dark portrait of MSU's nerdy underworld ("The devil would be at home in the Michigan State netherworld of tunnels," writes Dear); it also conveys the depth of Dallas's involvement with the game. "There's nothing to constrain you except the limit of your imagination," the boy told Dear. "When I played a character, I *was* the character." However, the book also depicts the game's positive aspects; if anything, it shows how helpful—not harmful—D&D was to Dallas. "Didn't bring all my personal problems along with me," he explained further. "It's a terrific escape." Far from a condemnation of D&D, *The Dungeon Master* is actually a cautionary tale about letting kids be kids, about not putting too much pressure on young adults—in short, about not sending a sixteen-year-old child to college. "Except for Dallas's parents and a few scattered acquaintances," the author writes, "no one had tried to guide the boy's potential intelligently." The missing person in Dear's book is not a menacing sociopath but a scared, lonely kid. Domineered by parents who pushed him too hard, Dallas responded by disappearing.[35]

Reports of more deaths—this time a double suicide by brothers in Colorado—mingled with the media furor surrounding Dear's book to build the D&D mystique even more.[36] The following spring, news of another suicide in Putnam, Connecticut, by thirteen-year-old Roland Cartier, who regularly played D&D, triggered debate about whether the game should be allowed in school. Criticisms became sharper, the language more accusatory. "It is another of Satan's ploys to pollute and destroy our children's minds," said one parent at a board of education meeting at Putnam High School. "You have authorized Russian roulette," said Rev. Robert Bakke, pastor of the Faith Bible Evangelical Free Church. "Over the months to come there will be many thrilling and harmless clicks of the gun as Dungeons and Dragons is held to the heads of our young people," he told the board. "But another deadly explosion will come." But investigator Paul Roy blamed drug use and a troubled home life, saying, "Dungeons and Dragons no way killed this kid." Those closest to the victim seemed to agree. "I'm sick of them saying that Roland killed himself because it was D&D," said Erik Bergeson, who played with Cartier. The fourteen-year-old added, "It was drugs."[37]

Dungeons and Dragons had become a cause célèbre for some conservative watchdog groups, a scapegoat for Christian fundamentalists, and a key point of contention in the culture wars of the 1980s. Patricia Pulling, Bink's grieving mother, founded BADD (Bothered about Dungeons and Dragons), calling the game "brainwashing" and a form of sacrilege. Portraying the game as an unhealthy obsession, the National Coalition on Television Violence (NCTV) linked D&D to fifty teenage deaths. "The game causes young men to kill themselves and others," asserted Dr. Thomas Radecki, a psychiatrist and chairman of the NCTV. Others defended the game. The Association for Gifted/Creative Children found that it encouraged reading; director Steven Spielberg used the game to measure young actors' role-playing abilities while casting the film *E.T.* The psychologist Joyce Brothers saw no harm in the game, and TSR maintained that it was no more reasonable to assume that youths would kill themselves after playing D&D than it was to assume that they would bake themselves after reading "Hansel and Gretel." Through it all, the game grew in popularity. By 1985, D&D had sold eight million copies and spun off a popular cartoon show on Saturday-morning television.[38]

When news reports turned from suicides to homicides, criticism of the game reached a crescendo. The *New York Times* publicized news of a shotgun slaying in late 1986 with the headline "16-Year-Old Is Convicted in Fantasy-Game Slaying of Boy, 11." In 1988, twenty-year-old college student Daniel Kasten was convicted in the shooting deaths of his parents at their Long Island home. He contended at the trial that his mind was under the control of a D&D character at the time of the slayings.[39]

Such negative attention never lessened its appeal to young people. D&D faded from the media spotlight in the 1990s, however, as newer electronic games began to displace the fantasy role-playing standby; these newer games attracted the attention of players and critics alike. In fact, if D&D diminished as a priority for Christian fundamentalists, then it did so largely because of the greater threat posed by video games. No longer the national craze it had been in the 1980s, D&D never lost favor in the gaming world, where hardcore players still rattle their polyhedron dice.

Interestingly, the same groups who criticized D&D also criticized video games; Radecki's National Coalition on Television Violence, for example, targeted both. Why? In what ways are fantasy role-playing games and electronic entertainment similar? How do they differ? The parallel between playing D&D and playing video games is made clear in one passage from William Dear's *The Dungeon Master*. "Someone watches those [television crime dramas] and thinks he can do the same thing," says Dear's assistant. "But here you're not watching, you're *doing*, at least in your imagination, and I think that could be a powerful force in your mind."[40] While "doing in your imagination" is an oxymoron of sorts, Dear's assistant clearly meant to suggest that there exists in gaming a certain degree of participation that supercedes the passivity of television watching. Both fantasy role-playing and video games share this sense of "doing." Video games arguably involve more doing; that is, more action takes place on-screen, at the control of the player, than in one's mind. Fantasy role-playing requires more imaginative engagement on the part of the player, more thinking and less button mashing.

One major difference between D&D worries and video game worries was that the former focused on suicide, the latter homicide. Those who worried about D&D seemed to focus on its antisocial aspects; the stories of the 1980s were stories of troubled teens and suicide. Whatever problems these teens had were directed toward the self—inward, not outward. The stories of the 1990s were, conversely, stories of alienated youths as first-person shooters: troubled teens who honed their shooting skills playing violent video games, then picked up real guns and used them with deadly accuracy. Eric Harris, before shooting up Columbine High School, referred to his favorite first-person-shooter video game in a videotaped confession intended to be publicized after the event. "It's going to be like fucking *Doom*," he gleefully anticipated. Lt. Col. David Grossman, among others, has marveled at how Michael Carneal, the fourteen-year-old who shot up a school in West Paducah, Kentucky, in 1997, achieved remarkable accuracy (eight shots, eight hits, on eight different victims) without ever having fired a real handgun; Carneal did, Grossman points out, play a lot of point-and-shoot video games.[41]

What's the difference between the hoopla over comic book hunts in the 1950s, D&D in the 1980s, and video games in the 1990s? School shootings, for one. The fear was that kids in the 1990s would harm others, and that video games would actually facilitate that harm—not only by desensitizing them as virtual killers but also by sharpening their marksmanship. Video games were making killing machines out of our nation's youth, Grossman persuasively argued. If anyone worried about video games leading to higher numbers of suicides among youth, those fears were kept private.

Of course, just as the overwhelming majority of kids who played Dungeons and Dragons did not commit suicide, the overwhelming majority of kids who play video games do not go on killing sprees. This fact suggests that those students who did kill themselves may have been troubled in other ways, and that those who kill others may be influenced by more than playing video games. Proponents of D&D touted how safe its dungeons really were. "It allows for all kinds of mental activity to take place in a safe environment," said Nicholas Long, a psychologist and director of the Rose School. "As long as it's not taken to extreme, this kind of fantasy can provide a rich inner life." Long continued, "A child who plays Dungeons & Dragons can have the same level of adventure—in his mind—as a nineteenth-century child might have in real life as an apprentice on a ship crossing the Atlantic." It is also important to note that one's inner world is only as safe as the environs of one's mind. It is likely that at least a few players in the 1980s did not encounter new demons in imaginary dungeons so much as they brought their own with them into the realm of D&D.[42]

Violent Video Games

The controversy over video games which began in the 1990s continues today. Like Dungeons and Dragons, violent video games have their defenders, and a compelling case can be made for their relative harmlessness. The main values of playing video games are self-evident. They allow role-playing and fantastic escapism. They build problem-solving skills and strengthen hand-eye coordination. They are a pleasant diversion—a distraction from the mundane—and most of all, they are fun.

James Paul Gee, professor of reading at the University of Wisconsin at Madison and author of *Why Video Games Are Good for the Soul* (2005), argues that video games capably blend learning and pleasure, while offering players an opportunity to script an outcome. "Players coauthor games by playing them," he writes, describing how good games allow players to feel like heroes and heroines in their own life stories.[43] One could take such arguments further, arguing that even (or especially) violent video games warrant serious consideration as positive, beneficial pastimes. In what other context can one actively role-play a star fighter or a gangster or a gunslinger, bludgeoning and blasting his way through waves of ghoulish bad guys? In what other context can one create such mayhem and carnage—only to wipe the screen clean with a push of the "Reset" button?

Recent studies have highlighted the benefits of playing video games—everything from boosting vocabulary, reasoning, and social skills in children to sharpening the laparoscopic surgery skills of young surgeons.[44] Yet, while certain studies, often publicized in industry magazines, have begun to point out the positive effects of video games, public concern regarding the potential harm of violent video games, confirmed by a growing body of research, still tends to dominate any discussion of the pluses and minuses of gaming. For example, two articles in the April 2000 issue of the *Journal of Personality and Social Psychology* noted that playing violent video games can increase a person's aggressive thoughts, feelings, and actions both in laboratory settings and outside of them.[45]

While there is no consistent empirical evidence to support the contentions that violent video games teach children how to kill, remove the natural hesitancy associated with killing, or provide youth with a desire to kill, there are, according to one expert, "noteworthy links" between violent video game play and aggressive behavior in youth.[46] In this regard, watching television and playing video games are similar. It is clear that heavy television viewing and prolonged video game playing have the same effect with regard to heightened aggression; what is not known is whether children come to mimic the violence they see because they think it is socially acceptable or whether troubled kids reinforce their behavioral patterns by viewing so much violence. Regardless, there is cause for concern, and the findings of scholars working today in this field seem to validate the concerns of Arthur Schlesinger Jr., who noted forty years ago that exposure to the spectacle of violence might create insensitivity, condition emotion and behavior, and attenuate people's sense of reality.[47]

Catharsis

As with violent entertainment in general, much of the argument for the positive effects of video games hinges on the notion of catharsis: the idea that viewing theatric violence can somehow dispel negative emotions. The notion of catharsis was first explored by Aristotle, who disagreed with his teacher Plato about the harm of seeing violence. Plato had argued that any harmful or violent image added to the sum of harm or violence in the world; therefore, no good could come from it. Many Greek tragedians seemingly agreed with Plato because they scripted their violence offstage (*ob scena*, in ancient Greek); they felt that it was not imperative for the audience to see the violent act occur. The audience, for example, never actually sees Oedipus blind himself after learning of his incestuous transgression: he wanders blindly back onto the stage, moaning and clutching his eyes after committing the "obscene" act.

Aristotle argued that dramatic violence serves a purpose beyond narrative advancement—that, in fact, viewing theatric violence could purge negative emotions such as fear, anxiety, pity, or sorrow. Poetry, plays, music, and speeches can have powerful emotional effects when essentially good characters are placed in situations that elicit fear and pity for them. Others have advanced similar theories, including William James and Sigmund Freud, who argued that watching violence allows accumulated aggression to "vent," leaving one emotionally calm.

Athletic competitions, particularly team sports, make the greatest claim to cathartic value. Because athletic competition involves animosity that can explode into hostility, it can also create tensions capable of intensifying the enjoyment of play; however, it is important to note that watching sports and playing them are two different things. Jeffrey Goldstein has written in his book *Why We Watch: The Attractions of Violent Entertainment* (1998),

> Whether or not a propensity to commit acts of physical aggression is an ineradicable part of "human nature," as Konrad Lorenz and countless others seem to believe, no one can doubt that men and, to a lesser degree, women have a millennia-long history of aggressiveness. It is the cherished belief of many sportswriters that sports and sports specta-torship are a means to rechannel this aggressiveness and to bring it to a harmless catharsis. . . . Unfortunately, the theory of catharsis, which may indeed be valid for those who experience "the pity and the terror" of tragic drama, has been thoroughly disconfirmed for the sports spectator.[48]

He goes on to cite a number of studies by social psychologists that support this claim. For example, two similar studies of sports fans at the University of Maryland in the late 1960s concluded that "the viewing of violent or aggressive acts tends to increase the aggressiveness of the viewer"; other studies in the 1970s and 1980s reached similar conclusions.[49] If playing sports can channel aggression and dispel it through competition, then watching sports yields far different results. How does one explain the now customary destruction by fans of the downtown area of whatever city is unlucky enough to win the Super Bowl or an NBA title? Where is the catharsis?

Video games are particularly interesting with regard to catharsis theory because the player is only partly participating, operating on a middle ground between active participation and passive observation. In this sense, video games might fall somewhere between playing sports and watching film. With a low participation-observation quotient, video games would seemingly reveal much about whatever cathartic value electronic media offers; accordingly, much of the research regarding violent video games has focused on how aggressive one feels before and after playing. This research, unfortunately, does not validate catharsis theory as related to video games. Craig Anderson, Douglas Gentile, and Katherine Buckley, authors of *Violent Video Game Effects on Children and Adolescents: Theory, Research, and Public Policy* (2007), maintain that violent video games, apart from whatever positive benefits they may hold, do not serve to "blow off steam." They write,

> There have been hundreds of studies of media violence—most of which could be interpreted as studies of catharsis. For example, in the studies reported here, children could have had lower aggressive thoughts and behaviors after playing the violent video games. However, they did not. This pattern is also found in most other studies of media violence. . . . Therefore, hundreds of studies demonstrate that people become more aggressive after consuming media violence, not less.[50]

Anderson, Gentile, and Buckley suggest that for catharsis to work in a Freudian sense, a person must experience increasing pressure to engage in a particular activity. For example, if a person does not eat, he will get hungrier and hungrier, and if he still does not eat, he will die. However, if a person does not aggress, he does not get more aggressive, nor does he die from lack of aggressing; therefore, aggression is not a drive, and it cannot lead to catharsis. Viewing, thinking about, or performing aggressive acts tends to increase later aggressive behavior, not reduce it—in part because repeating experiences is one of the most effective ways to learn something. Practice makes perfect, and if one "practices" aggressive thoughts, feelings, and responses, it cannot lead to lowered aggressive thoughts, feelings, and responses over time.

The case for the cathartic value of television violence is even weaker. Writing on the subject, Victor C. Strasburger and

Barbara J. Wilson bluntly state, "The scientific evidence . . . shows that media violence has quite the opposite effect than that which is predicted by catharsis. . . . In over forty years of research, *there has been no substantiation of the catharsis theory*."[51] Steven J. Kirsh, author of *Children, Adolescents, and Media Violence: A Critical Look at the Research* (2006), agrees, writing, "For the past fifty years, not only has research consistently failed to empirically support the catharsis effect, but frequently the opposite effect has been found, in that aggressive experiences result in increases in aggressive behavior." He finds that violent media increases not only aggression but also anxiety: "Research on adults suggests that as the level of video game violence increases, so too does the player's level of anxiety."[52] Interestingly, some catharsis may occur in viewing horror films, which people see in order to experience in safety emotions that are usually associated with danger, such as fear and anxiety. It provides a safe outlet for unsafe emotions. However, whatever benefit might be gained in watching such films may be offset by the increasingly graphic violence depicted in many of them. If the distance between fantasy and reality allows the mental space to process visual depictions of violence—cathartically or otherwise—then what happens when that distance is deliberately erased through increasingly graphic renderings of horror and gore?

Green Blood

Films may be read as cultural artifacts, indicative of the society that brings them into being, and the spate of torture films in the first years of the twenty-first century—*Saw, Hostel, Turistas, Captivity*—seemed to reflect the nation's fascination with and ambivalence toward the Bush administration's condoning of torture in Iraq and elsewhere. A pair of morally flexible vigilante films—*The Brave One*, starring Jodie Foster, and *Death Sentence*, starring Kevin Bacon—similarly reflected an attempt to reconcile some sort of societal angst, perhaps the free-floating anxiety of the post-9/11 world. "The reason I wanted to do it was because of the kind of nameless fears people in Western society have at the moment," said Neil Jordan, director of *The Brave One*. "If I was tapping into anything, I was tapping into that." What stood out to many reviewers, however, was not the cultural relevance of *The Brave One* and *Death Sentence* but rather what one writer termed their "blood-spattering" violence, "as subtle as a shotgun blast to the face."[53]

The issue is not that films such as *Saw* or *Hostel* are exceedingly violent (which they are) nor even that they mark a sick zenith of sadism (which they do). Rather the issue is whether or not the heightened realism of these films represents something new in Hollywood: a pinnacle of representational gore. On the one hand, since the final scene of Edwin Porter's classic western *The Great Train Robbery* (1903), in which an outlaw fires his Colt .45 point-blank at the audience, there has never been a time when critics have not lamented an upsurge in dangerously convincing cinematic violence. The outcry in the 1920s over gangster films and the glamorization of outlawry brought into existence the Hays Code; nonetheless, complaints about the lack of authenticity in American films led to the end of the production code in the 1960s, when an upswing in cinematic violence caused even louder howls of protest. Films such as Arthur Penn's *Bonnie and Clyde* (1967) and Sam Peckinpah's *The Wild Bunch* (1969) redefined screen violence during this period; these films in turn were supplanted by newer films that upped the ante. To titillate, to shock, and to fill seats, filmmakers strived for greater realism. The violence has climbed steadily, faithfully reproduced while seeming quite real to audiences. Therefore, violence—the hallmark of American cinema—always seems to be in the process of becoming more lifelike and evocative.[54]

On the other hand, one could argue that contemporary cinematography has rendered Hollywood violence largely indistinguishable from the real thing. Today's films can make the greatest claim to graphic realism, as filmmakers strive to bring the grittiest of realities to the big (and little) screen. Perhaps more than any other dramatic element, theatric violence has benefited from the special effects and technological advancements of the digital age to create the most genuine, lifelike, and convincing depictions of body trauma and gruesome death.

Such violence can be serious, compelling, and beautiful, as evidenced by one of the most popular movies of the turn of the century, Steven Spielberg's *Saving Private Ryan* (1998), as well as one of the most anticipated, Mel Gibson's *The Passion of the Christ* (2004); such violence can also be graphic, brutal, and extreme, as evidenced by these same films. While such films may have utilized new ways of making violence speak to audience members, they also threatened to make such renderings too vivid, too palpable, too real.

Cinematic history has been defined, as Philip French has observed, by the battle not only between moralists, reformers, and legislators on the one hand and filmmakers on the other, but also between the medium's greatest artists and its most blatant commercial exploiters.[55] The lines drawn in this second battle are not always easy to discern. Some of the most critically acclaimed directors of the last half of the twentieth century—Peckinpah, Penn, Oliver Stone, and others—pushed well beyond norms of cinematic violence in what they claimed to be parodies; in doing so, they may be accused of reveling in the very violence they sought to satirize.

While critics have skewered certain directors for their depictions of violence, the American public has been quick to forgive others, especially Spielberg. When the ABC network chose to broadcast *Saving Private Ryan* on November 11, 2004, in honor of Veterans Day, there was public outcry; however, the fuss centered on the film's coarse language. FCC regulators ruled that the film, which contains not only numerous expletives as part of the soldiers' dialogue but also extreme graphic violence, did not violate indecency guidelines. The FCC said its decency and profanity guidelines were not applicable to violent programming. Nonetheless, sixty-six ABC affiliates, skittish over the film's expletives, decided not to air the film; these affiliates covered nearly a third of the national viewing audience. Those who could access it watched the film reverently, in seeming agreement with FCC chairman Michael Powell. "This film is a critically acclaimed artwork that tells a gritty story—one of bloody battles and supreme heroism," Powell noted. "The horror of war and the enormous personal sacrifice it draws on cannot be painted in airy pastels."[56]

One wonders what James Agee might have said about the American public's generally enthusiastic reception of *Saving Private Ryan*. Writing about war documentaries for *Fortune* magazine in 1945, Agee concluded that "we have no business seeing this sort of experience except through our presence and participation."

> If at an inscrutable distance from participation, hopelessly incapable of reactions adequate to the event, we watch men killing each other, we may be quite as profoundly degraded ourselves and, in the process, betraying and separating ourselves the farther from those we are trying to identify ourselves with; none the less because we tell ourselves sincerely that we sit in comfort and watch carnage in order to nurture our patriotism, our conscience, our understanding and our sympathies.[57]

As Michael Leach has written, "War is certainly a far greater obscenity than the movies that glorify it, but that doesn't make the latter any less obscene."[58]

The fear is that, regardless of directorial intent, the mind sees what the mind sees, and in a world of perfectly spurting blood squibs and carefully reconstructed gore, there is little separation between the representation of a violent act and the act itself. That separation lies, more often than not, in the critical apparatus of the viewer—but if a valid argument against pornographic movies is that they distort reality by taking the part (i.e., physical sexuality) and making it the whole, then how should we perceive movies that treat human beings as meat grenades, ready to explode in not-so-fake blood? One could argue that the synecdoche of pornography applies as much to violence as it does to sex, insofar as human beings are (quite literally) reduced to bits and pieces.

Steven J. Kirsh has described his own unsatisfying experience of playing a video game in which zombies, when shot, die in pools of green blood. While craving greater realism from the game, Kirsh recognizes that, in order not to violate decency standards and to market the game to children, "virtual blood needs to run green."[59] Another reason (which Kirsh does not fully explain) is that people likely *need* some sort of separation between real violence and fantasy violence. Children certainly do, and today's toy makers have attempted to maintain that distinction by replacing realistic toy guns with non-black, brightly colored ones.

As with cartoons and children's play, a crucial distinction must be made between fantasy violence and realistic violence. When realism "bleeds" into fantasy—that is, when we find ourselves enthralled and even entertained by increasingly realistic forms of violence—then the risk to mental and spiritual well-being increases, regardless of the medium, regardless of what the creator intended, and regardless of whether the viewer/participant is a child or an adult. Realistic depictions of violence are increasingly indistinguishable from the real thing, and—as with video games—this line between fantasy and reality becomes even more important as it thins, wavers, and threatens to disappear.[60]

Of course, there is a darker, more disturbing possibility— that distinctions between fake and real matter little when assessing the effects of violent imagery. Each of us has only one pair of eyes, which funnel information to the visual cortex of a single brain. It is not as if multiple sets of eyes process fictive and real visual stimuli separately, or neurons automatically filter and separate images into categories of fictive or real. Brains process a constant stream of imagery, some "real," some manufactured and mediated. Is that which *seems* real processed differently from that which is unquestionably real, or do they pool together in the strange inner workings of the mind? It is this latter possibility to which St. Augustine alluded when he suggested that seeing violence—*any* kind of violence—is akin to stabbing the soul. If the mind sees what the mind sees, then it is very difficult to moderate violent imagery before, during, or even after it has been filed away in the banks of memory.

Do distinctions between real and unreal matter? Of course they do—but knowing something is make-believe can have little bearing on attitudes, beliefs, and decision making. Jaws was an animatronic robot (named, somewhat reassuringly, Bruce) who scared a generation of kids out of the ocean. Adults know that advertisements are fake yet ads still influence consumer buying habits. While developmental psychology suggests that children do not understand the concepts of pretend and real in the same way as adults, different studies involving college students have found significant increases in aggression as a result of exposure to cartoonish violent media; these findings suggest that neither age nor an advanced ability to distinguish between fantasy and reality protect one from media effects. If sound, then such findings point to an alternate and unnerving (but ultimately unsurprising) truth—that adults, not just children, are at risk if they imbibe too much violence.

CHAPTER 3

Gun Crazy

The United States is said to be the greatest gun-toting nation in the world. It has the reputation of there being more murders committed in its boundaries annually than in all the countries of Europe combined, and most of these crimes are committed with guns. It is said that there is one murder committed in this country every forty minutes, and over nine thousand each year. . . . Seemingly, the pistol is one of the most popular playthings in America today.
— New York State Crime Commission, 1929

As a nation that is clearly unbalanced, the United States should not be surprised when some of its citizens reflect this unbalance to an excessive degree.
— Robert Sherrill, *The Saturday Night Special* (1973)

The Gun Culture

Around the world, people own guns because they have to. They are a necessary unpleasantness of daily life in some war-torn corners of the globe. Here in the United States people own guns because they want to. Appreciating that fundamental difference allows a better understanding of Americans' fascination with firearms and the proliferation of firearms in this nation.

American citizens have always had firearms, and guns have always been a part of American society. "The origins of gun use in America are honorable," writes Jervis Anderson in *Guns in American Life* (1984), which describes the advent of the gun culture in the United States. The colonists used them not only to put meat on their tables but also to win independence from the British. Early American settlers used them for sustenance and for survival. Included in the Bill of Rights, firearms had not only political connotations but also racial ones: as an instrument of white settlers, guns came to represent a safeguard and passkey to citizenship. "The early, necessary reliance upon the gun lasted for some time, as the nation grew and expanded westward," Anderson writes. "But long after the weapon had ceased to be indispensable to domestic survival and nation-building, generations of Americans continued to embrace and glorify it as a living inheritance—as a permanent ingredient of the nation's style and culture."[1] It is this aspect of American firearms—their living inheritance, rooted in history and dignified in political culture—that animates and sustains the gun culture today.

The relatively simple origins of American gun use have developed into a comparatively complex gun culture that means different things in different places. In different regions of the country guns serve different purposes; as a result, gun ownership and gun use carry different connotations in different locales. In some rural areas, for example, guns are still everyday tools, used to scare away pests or predators and to hunt for game. In suburban areas, guns can be more recreational, used for target shooting and plinking. In urban areas, gun use is darkly social, used for self-protection and committing crimes. Accordingly, attitudes toward guns are not largely a partisan issue but rather a geographical one.

Similarly, the reasons why people buy guns to keep in their homes, in their cars, or on their person are as varied as their owners. People report keeping a gun for hunting, target shooting, and personal protection. Among those who own handguns, 75 percent reported that self-protection is the primary reason for owning a firearm, according to a national survey in 1996.[2] If they were once likely to venture into the woods for game, Americans are now more likely to shoot animals with a camera than with a gun: hunting, a traditional excuse for keeping a firearm, has declined in popularity—particularly among young people. A 1995 survey by the National Shooting Sports Foundation found that only 25 percent of hunters were under the age of thirty-five, down from 48 percent a decade earlier.[3]

Perceived need plays a large role in the proliferation of guns. Personal protection and fear of crime inspire many gun owners, but other reasons still factor into the calculus of gun ownership, particularly in the South and the Rocky Mountain region, where gun ownership is highest. In a 2006 essay for *Harper's* magazine, Garret Keizer describes the region where he grew up and the people who live there:

> They have guns because they hunt for meat, and they have guns for the same reason that many of them also have ponds dug close to their barns and houses. In a community with no fire hydrants, you want water for the fire engine. And in an area where a handful of state police and part-time sheriffs patrol a vast web of back roads spread across three counties, you might want the means to defend yourself. I own a fire extinguisher, a first-aid kit, and a shotgun. Not to own any of these would strike me as an affectation.[4]

In Keizer's community, like many others, gun owning speaks to a very American kind of self-reliance. "Owning a gun does not enhance my sense of power; it enhances my sense of compromise and contingency—a feeling curiously like that of holding down a job," he writes. "In other words, it is one more glaring proof that I am not Mahatma Gandhi or even Che Guevara, just another soft-bellied schlimazel trying to keep the lawn mowed and the psychopaths off the lawn." He admits a kind of tension between gun ownership and powerlessness, or what he calls "the illusion of power and choice perpetuated to disguise a diminishing sphere of action."[5]

The numbers of gun owners belie the strength of the gun culture, in part because "gun culture" is more than a descriptor for the small but not insignificant number of Americans who own guns: it is the sum of gun owners and nonowners alike, coping with a web of attitudes, beliefs, customs, policies, and laws related to firearms and their related industries. It is surprising, perhaps, to know that a minority of Americans actually own guns; in fact, one in four American adults currently own a gun of some kind, according to one researcher. Approximately 40 percent of adult males and 10 percent of adult females are gun owners. At the same time, according to one expert, local, state, regional, and national polls have been "fairly consistent from year to year" in showing that "a strong majority" favors gun control laws; this majority has tended to increase slightly every few years.[6] Many gun owners may be included in this group. Attitudes about gun control are more complicated than simply who owns guns and who does not: if the majority of American men and women do not own guns, then many non-owners accept the right of others to keep firearms—just as many gun owners are open to reasonable gun control measures. Such is the gun culture, of which every American is a part.[7]

The British Are Coming

The origins of American gun culture are wrapped in history, steeped in folklore and legend. From the very beginnings of colonial American history, Americans used firearms to tame an untamed land; ever since then, the base utility of firearms has easily blended with the romantic imagination of a people enthralled with the origins of a nation. It is hard to imagine the Puritans without their trumpet-shaped blunderbusses as they stepped with trepidation into what they saw as an ominous wilderness. It is even harder to imagine the Minutemen of Lexington and Concord without their muskets at hand, ready to repel the insidious British redcoats in and around Boston. Firearms were used to harvest game and to defend against hostile Indians and wild animals. They were used in equal parts to hunt and protect, and they joined other implements as unpretentious necessities of pioneer life. If the ax cleared the virgin timber of the eastern woodlands and the plow made the land useful for homesteading, then the muzzleloader held at bay a rough country that threatened to encroach on the only kind of progress the first Americans knew and valued. The firearms they used have come to embody the spirit of self-reliance that Americans cherish.

In peacetime and in war, individual makes and models of

firearms have become almost totemic: the Kentucky rifle, used by Daniel Boone, Davy Crockett, and other pioneers against "bars and Injuns" in the backwoods of Kentucky and Tennessee; the Sharps carbine, the reliable breechloader favored by Civil War cavalrymen; the .44-40 Henry rifle, castigated by Confederate soldiers as "that damned Yankee rifle that you load on Sunday and shoot all week"; the Winchester repeating rifle, the "Gun That Tamed the West"; the Colt Peacemaker, the "Great Equalizer" of the western frontier; the Thompson submachine gun (or "tommy gun"), used by gangsters and lawmen alike during Prohibition; the .45 Colt automatic pistol, strapped to the sides of American servicemen through two World Wars and beyond. Such weapons have come to represent the ideals and values of those who wielded them. They represent freedom, bravery, individualism, and democracy itself.

Americans have imbued these guns with a romantic mysticism that far surpasses their pragmatic utility as tools and weapons, and this adoration feeds a kind of fetishistic enthusiasm that couples today's gun culture with yesterday's. The guns serve as a kind of conduit to the metanarrative of American history; that is, by owning a firearm one is tied to the Minutemen, soldiers, and cowboys glorified in U.S. history. This connection, in conjunction with the Second Amendment, has helped to create a gun culture in which many Americans have the desire to own a gun, not only as their right but as a way of tapping into history. It is perhaps not surprising then that thousands of Americans each year flock to reenactments of historic battles at Gettysburg and other Civil War sites; that others participate in fast-growing "cowboy action shooting" events, which include quick-draw competitions; and that many gun enthusiasts collect antique firearms and modern replicas even as they trade for the newest high-tech weaponry.

If Americans now recognize some of the sinister uses of these same firearms in American history, then we still choose to favor the gun as a symbol of American might and right. While Jervis Anderson may be correct about the honorable origins of American gun use, he also overlooks how settlers used them to depopulate animal species (including some hunted to extinction), to enslave and disenfranchise African Americans, and to war against hostile and peaceable Native Americans alike. There are many heroic and romantic representations of guns in American history; however, the history of American gun use would be incomplete without acknowledging these other uses too.

Gun Fun

It is hard to ignore the prominent place of firearms in American history and mythology. It is also hard to ignore that guns are, for a majority of the populace, much less utilitarian than they once were—they are now more of a recreational toy than a necessity of daily life for most individuals. Hunting is no longer a necessary means of feeding one's family. A scant few of us— namely law enforcement personnel, security guards, ranchers, and perhaps small business owners in high-crime areas—have a legitimate need for firearms. An argument can also be made for those in rural communities without many law enforcement personnel, but such folks are still in the minority. The fact remains that most Americans do not regularly *need* firearms—yet a number of citizens own them. Many people arm themselves as a deterrent against crime, but FBI crime reports demonstrate a decrease in violent crime since 1994; therefore, it follows that fewer people need to arm themselves. In the great paradox of American gun owning, however, a heightened desire for guns trumps diminishing necessity: more Americans want to keep a gun when there is demonstrably less need to have one.

If hunting has diminished in popularity, and if crime rates have dropped, then how might the strength of the gun culture and the health of the gun industry be explained? It should be clear that need only plays a small role in the desire of many Americans—particularly males—to own a gun. People *want* guns, which fill a psychological craving sustained by the media, popular culture, and various forms of entertainment. Americans are encouraged to believe that guns create certain options for those who wield them. Guns allow otherwise weak individuals to impose their will on their environment. Donald Newman learned from interviews in the California prison system that criminals enjoy that imposition as much as anyone else. "The most important element in robbery often was not the acquisition of money," he wrote of his interviewees, "but the one brief moment in which these men held a gun and forced someone to do anything they commanded."[8] For those who walk the straight and narrow, no less than for criminals, guns serve as a kind of buffer against the uncertainties and contingencies of life in postmodern America, maintaining the "illusion of power and choice" described by Keizer. They seem to afford a degree of control in an out-of-control world, and regardless of whether people are actually any safer when armed, many certainly seem to *feel* safer. That the presence of a gun may actually increase the chance of violence is rarely considered.

Wanting a gun is bolstered by the omnipresence of firearms in popular entertainment, especially movies and television. One cannot overestimate how guns function as a kind of fantasy prop in American culture and society, and Hollywood has done its part to exalt firearms. Movie stars and television actors use guns to right wrongs, to combat injustice, and to thwart criminals. John Wayne, Clint Eastwood, and other screen idols have helped to define a masculinity that is quick with a gun and economical with words. The Great American Hero shoots straight, both figuratively and literally, and this archetype defines gender roles insofar as American men imagine themselves in a tradition of independence, self-sufficiency, and ruggedness, perhaps even emulating what they see on-screen. Antiheroes, too, glorify the gun, as rappers extol the virtues of the "gat" and Tony Montana invites us to "say 'ello to mah leetle frend" as he brandishes an M-16 with attached grenade launcher in Brian de Palma's *Scarface* (1983). In this way, movies and entertainment—like history—play a role in sustaining the gun culture.

In such a context, it is easy to see guns as not only necessary but also enjoyable, and the enjoyment of guns is inculcated at an early age. Aggressive play may be nearly universal among young males, but American boys in particular are raised to revere and admire the gun culture. Toy guns, play violence, and games such as cops and robbers, cowboys and Indians, and "army" imbue a certain fascination with firearms. While more study is needed, researchers have found that playing with toy guns leads to more aggressive play; with significant gender differences, it can also influence aggressive behavior.[9]

Such play can have dire consequences. Realistic toy guns were pulled from shelves in the 1970s after a number of instances in which police officers fired on children with fake guns, mistaking them in low-light conditions for actual weapons. Since passage of the Federal Toy Gun Law by Congress in 1988, toy guns now come with bright-orange muzzles, but realistic-looking "Airsoft" guns—black replicas that fire plastic BBs—have again renewed concerns over toy guns. In February 2007, Gander Mountain replaced realistic replica guns, which accounted for $3.5 million in Gander sales in 2006, with unmistakable toys in its 105 retail stores. Other nations have gone further, recognizing the importance of limiting children's exposure to guns, even toy guns. In January 2009, for example, Mexico's National Assembly debated a legislative ban on the fabrication, importation, and sale of toy guns and other warlike toys. It was one of a number of legislative proposals aimed at addressing an explosion of killings and kidnappings, many of them tied to narcotics traffickers fighting with authorities for control of lucrative transit routes.[10]

It is unclear to what degree toy guns feed children's interest in actual firearms, but many adults certainly enjoy playing with guns. Just as children have their toys, adults do too, and few gun enthusiasts would deny that shooting is fun. Aligning the sights, drawing a bead, squeezing the trigger, hearing the satisfying *crack* of a rifle or *boom* of a shotgun, smelling the burnt gunpowder, hitting one's mark . . . all are part of the special joys of shooting. Whether raised in a gun household (which is the greatest predictor of adult gun owning, according to one expert) or not, a significant proportion of Americans buy guns, sell them, trade them, collect them, fieldstrip them, clean them, polish them, display them, and shoot them.[11] They appreciate the craftsmanship and beauty of guns, and happily debate the flaws and merits of particular designs. All are important aspects of the shooting sports, in which enthusiasts shoot guns in the same way other people play golf or tennis.

The uses of guns in recreation are myriad, translating into big bucks. As of 2007, there were 17 million "active target shooters" in the United States, according to the National

Shooting Sports Foundation (NSSF), which defines active target shooters as people who have participated in skeet, trap, sporting clays, or target shooting in the past year; 10.7 million participate in handgun target shooting. The NSSF estimates that American shooters spent approximately $2.1 billion in 2005 on firearms and ammunition—a figure imperfectly calculated by back-projecting excise taxes on sales. If figures from the NSSF are an indicator, then hunting has become an increasingly expensive pastime, in which hunters spend an average $1,896 per year on trucks, boats, gas, food, lodging, apparel, and gear, for a total of $2.7 billion.[12]

American Roulette

Americans are fairly unique in the sheer number of guns circulating in their society. Compared to citizens in other high-income nations, Americans own more guns, particularly handguns. These guns are not evenly distributed, as they increasingly find their way into the hands of collectors and enthusiasts; owners of four or more guns—about 10 percent of the adult population—are in possession of 77 percent of the total U.S. stock of firearms. The increase in urbanization and the decline in hunting, combined with the fact that fewer adults live in each household, have resulted in a decreasing percentage of households with firearms, according to scholars; the number of households with long guns (rifles and shotguns) fell from 40 percent in 1973 to 32 percent in 1994.[13] Still, while estimates of the total number of guns are imperfect, there are upward of 225 million guns circulating in American society, with more being made each year. According to the Bureau of Alcohol, Tobacco, and Firearms (ATF), American manufacturers made 3,079,517 guns in 2004, including 728,511 pistols, 294,099 revolvers, 1,325,138 rifles, and 731,769 shotguns. Of these, 132,509 were exported, leaving 2,947,008 new guns for domestic sale. Notably, the kind of guns Americans own has changed. While the number of households with handguns has apparently declined since the mid-1990s, with new handgun sales shrinking by more than half a million between 1989 and 1996, the dominant handguns in the current market have been medium- and large-caliber semiautomatic pistols designed as combat weapons (the same guns most often featured in Hollywood and TV crime dramas). Perhaps 16 percent of U.S. adults currently own handguns, most of which—despite some adaptations for target and hunting use—are primarily intended for use against humans at close range.[14]

All of these guns, not surprisingly, affect the levels of gun violence in this society—and not for the better. Where it is easier to obtain a gun, it is also easier to be shot: the more guns, the more gun violence, whether accidental or deliberate. With the highest rate of gun ownership in the world—about one gun per citizen—the United States also has the highest rate of gun death and injury of any industrialized nation. In 1997, for example, over 32,000 Americans died of gunshot wounds—more than died from AIDS or liver disease in that same year. The death rate by firearms in the United States is not the highest in the world—Columbia, for example, has a higher one—but it exceeds that of any other developed nation by a wide margin; rates of gun violence in the United States are so high that even people who are at relatively low risk by American standards are "at risk" by international standards. While youth crime rates in the early twenty-first century receded a bit, in the late 1990s gunshots threatened to overtake car accidents, fires, and the like as the leading cause of death by injury, according to the Centers for Disease Control and Prevention (CDC); in 2006, homicide by firearm was the second leading cause of injury death among Americans between the ages of ten and twenty-four.[15]

The goriest video game pales in comparison to the reality of cinema verité, but both pale in comparison to the bloody reality of guns in American life: the statistics for gun homicide are as jaw-dropping as they are ugly. Between 1991 and 2000, forty Americans were murdered with guns on an average day. Since 1960, approximately 500,000 Americans have been murdered with guns. Casualties of war help to put this number in perspective: more Americans have been murdered with guns in the past forty years than were killed in all wars in the twentieth century—in World War I, World War II, the Korean War, the Vietnam War, and the Gulf War combined.[16]

Accidents account for two to three firearms deaths every

day in the United States. Most are self-inflicted; most are caused by handguns, which are easy to point in an unsafe direction; and most occur during routing gun handling, such as cleaning, loading, and unloading. For every unintentional firearm fatality, it is estimated that approximately thirteen victims are injured seriously enough to be treated in hospital emergency rooms; in other words, every day more than thirty Americans are unintentionally and nonfatally shot by themselves or by someone else.[17]

Such figures do not account for deliberately self-inflicted gunshots, which are even higher. Since 1965, more than half a million Americans have committed suicide with a firearm, nearly ten times as many as have died from gun-related accidents. Almost fifty people each day kill themselves with guns in the United States—more than by all other methods of suicide combined. Guns facilitate killing oneself in the same way they facilitate killing others: among methods of suicide, firearms are typically the most lethal.[18]

As a major producer of firearms and a major source of illegal arms, the United States is also a key contributor to gun violence in other nations. American-made guns not only kill U.S. citizens but also jeopardize the safety of citizens in other nations, particularly those nearby. More firearm deaths occur in countries at peace than in those at war, and more than half of those are in the Americas, according to Wendy Cukier and Victor Sidel, authors of *The Global Gun Epidemic: From Saturday Night Specials to AK-47s* (2006), who call the United States a "flea market for every other nation's illegal gun market."[19] According to retired ATF agent Daniel McBride, "The United States has for many years been a warehouse, a shopping center, if you will, for firearms. . . . We are a very easy place from which to obtain firearms for transshipment back home."[20]

Guns, of course, are not necessary to perpetrate violence in the United States or anywhere else, and in this sense they do not necessarily equate with violence. Knives, fists, and clubs are common substitutes for guns in violent altercations; however, guns are noteworthy for several reasons. First, it is difficult to imagine certain kinds of violence without the involvement of guns. Would what happened at Columbine or Virginia Tech have been possible if the killers were not armed with guns—if the gunmen were not, in fact, gunmen? It is no coincidence that every president who has been wounded or killed in an assassination attempt was shot; as Arthur Schlesinger Jr. has written, "No one has ever tried to assassinate a President with a bow and arrow."[21] School shootings, assassination attempts, bank robberies, armored truck heists, and other crimes are inherently linked to guns. They are the weapons of choice for disgruntled youths and office workers aiming to kill a large number of classmates or coworkers in a short amount of time. As Philip J. Cook and Jens Ludwig observe, "We don't see drive-by knifings or innocent bystanders killed by stray fists."[22]

Second, guns intensify violence exponentially. More lethal than other handheld weapons, guns raise the stakes in any argument or confrontation. The lethality of guns makes the outcome of any violent encounter more likely to be death—of a participant or of a bystander. When people refer to the instrumentality or the functionality of firearms, it is this lethality to which they are referring—the deadly effectiveness, the killing power of guns. Without guns, people intent on harming someone else are still capable of injurious assault, at the very least, but with them, they are more likely to kill.

Third, guns facilitate violence with impersonal, point-and-shoot efficiency. Killing without a gun requires a sustained, physical commitment to murder, but guns kill at a distance, separating the killer from the bloody business of stabbing, bludgeoning, or using one's bare hands. Guns kill quickly, with little effort or risk to the shooter. They are easy to handle, easy to operate, and often easy to conceal and carry. In short, firearms enable those who could not or would not kill, who might otherwise lack the strength or will, to do so more readily.

These attributes exist apart from whatever criminal intent an armed person may have, and it is important to distinguish the problem of lethal violence from a generalized discussion of crime. American citizens often perceive that the United States has a crime problem; however, U.S. crime rates, as determined by victimization surveys, resemble those of other high-income nations. What sets the United States apart are a readiness and willingness to engage in potentially lethal violence, which is not necessarily a by-product of high levels of crime and large numbers of criminals. Americans are more likely to be shot in a traffic altercation or in a barroom fight than in a burglary. The reason for this truism is relatively simple: "crime" (that is, theft or robbery or burglary) oftentimes is not the motivation for committing violence. As Franklin E. Zimring and Gordon Hawkins have pointed out in *Crime Is Not the Problem: Lethal Violence in America* (1997), the United States does not have a crime problem so much as it has a *violence* problem, above and beyond whatever troubles it has with crime. They write, "What is striking about the quantity of lethal violence in the United States is that it is a third-world phenomenon occurring in a first-world nation."[23]

Of course, while assault is itself a crime, not all instances of gun violence can be considered assault (accidents or suicides, for example, cannot be considered assaults), even if most all uses of guns are violent. For this reason, it makes sense to disaggregate the issue of guns from crime, to discuss guns as specifically related to the violence they facilitate. Zimring and Hawkins make a convincing argument in *Crime Is Not the Problem*, adding evidence to a rather distressing possibility. The problem of American violence is made worse, perhaps, by an overabundance of firearms, by a willingness to use them freely against other people, and by what Jack Miles has called "the wildcat do-it-yourself policing of private gun ownership."[24]

The Secret Lives of Guns: Kids and Guns

Gun accidents and school shootings make the problem of gun violence particularly acute with regard to children. Young people are the primary victims in gun accidents. More than half of all unintentional firearm fatalities are individuals under the age of twenty-five. Although relatively few adolescents own guns, the fifteen-to-nineteen-year-old age group has (by far) the highest rate of unintentional firearm fatalities. American children under the age of fifteen are nine times as likely to die as a result of a fatal gun accident as same-age children in the rest of the developed world, according to the CDC.[25]

That the United States neither views guns in terms of consumer safety nor holds firearms to the same federal safety standards as other products speaks much about the strange place firearms occupy, stuck in a kind of nonregulated limbo—apart from other consumer goods—where they pose a unique danger to children. One could argue that guns are designed and intended to kill, and are therefore subject to different consumer-safety regulations than items without that purpose; however, one could also argue that firearms deserve special consideration expressly *because* they are designed to kill.

There is clearly a disconnect between the regulation of firearms and other products, such as appliances, power tools, and even toys. In September 2007, for example, toy maker Mattel recalled millions of Chinese-manufactured toys tainted with lead-contaminated paint; the recall followed other recalls during the previous months by other toy manufacturers, including Mattel's subsidiary, Fisher-Price. While no deaths or injuries were reported, the story dominated headlines, worried parents, and prompted congressional investigations—even as other children succumbed to accidental shooting deaths, including twelve-year-old Jazamine Wellisley of Ironwood, Michigan, on August 28; sixteen-year-old Robert Wilson Jr. of Alamogordo, New Mexico, on September 7; five-year-old Austin Gabriel Haley of Norman, Oklahoma, on September 9; fourteen-year-old Jakob Heath of Fort Bend, Texas, on September 17; two-year-old Cruzita Arellano of Ceres, California, on September 20; sixteen-year-old Larry Anthony Ballas of Tifton, Georgia, on September 23; and fifteen-year-old Quantrail Jameir Fox of Tulsa, Oklahoma, also on September 23. If governmental efforts and public awareness campaigns have greatly reduced the number of accidents that can befall children—including lead paint contamination, playground falls, swimming pool drownings, electric shock, poisoning by household cleansers, and even the possibility of entrapment in car trunks and old refrigerators—then they have yet to affect the problem of accidental shootings in comparable ways.[26]

Between 1982 and 1988, 3,607 children and teenagers (from zero to nineteen years old) died from unintentional firearm-related injuries, constituting 32 percent of all unintentional firearm-related deaths during this period, according to CDC statistics. Since 1988, the Eddie Eagle GunSafe Program of the National Rifle Association (NRA) has taught children from prekindergarten through sixth grade to avoid unsupervised guns: "If you see a gun: STOP! Don't touch. Leave the area. Tell an adult." The program has been used by 25,000 schools, civic groups, and law enforcement agencies to instruct more than twenty million children. It is hard to determine whether such efforts have reduced the numbers of accidental shootings, but the NRA certainly deserves credit for trying.[27]

Despite these efforts, the statistics regarding gun violence and children in the United States are still quite sobering, as reported by Ted Schwarz, author of *Kids and Guns: The History, the Present, the Dangers, and the Remedies* (1999). For example in 1995, one year after the passage of the Violent Crime Control and Law Enforcement Act and the Youth Handgun Safety Act, 3,280 children and teenagers were murdered with guns, another 1,450 committed suicide, and 440 died in accidental shootings, for a grand total of 5,170 young people killed by firearms, or about fourteen every day that year.[28] Schwarz broadly treats the liberal aspects of gun ownership in the United States that not only enable young people to access firearms but also create an atmosphere in which accidents can occur. He examines the gun-sale loopholes that have allowed consumers to purchase handguns without following the Brady Bill or the Instant Check System: loopholes such as estate sales and personal sales by so-called vest-pocket dealers, both of which seldom result in a record of transaction, a background check, or a report to any authority. He discusses a state law in Arizona that allows any adult to carry a handgun so long as it is visible to passersby. It is no more unusual in Arizona "to see motorcycle riders traveling from Phoenix to the Grand Canyon with a clearly visible revolver or automatic handgun in a shoulder holster" than it is to see openly armed people strolling the streets of Tombstone as if the gunfight at the O.K. Corral had occurred yesterday.[29] In such a world, the opportunities for accidents are many, whether a shooter is extensively trained or not. To illustrate, Schwarz describes a stress test conducted by the Phoenix Police Department designed to simulate a homeowner's experience of firing a bedside gun at night, under duress:

> The officer lay on a bed, his revolver on a nightstand, and then let himself relax, drifting off toward sleep. The room was

dark, but there was a light behind the closed bedroom door, and a human silhouette target was rigged to be visible when the door was opened.

Suddenly the door was opened, and the light from the hallway filled the bedroom. The officer came alert, grabbed his revolver, and fired six rounds of ammunition at the target designed to look like an armed intruder. How many times did this top handgun expert hit the target in the test simulating a homeowner's expected handgun use? Not one time.[30]

Such a test may not explain the preponderance of real-life incidents in which family members accidentally shoot other family members, but they may explain the limited utility of handguns for home defense by the average citizen.

It is worth noting that most of the people who own handguns are not criminals and indeed consider themselves to be responsible individuals. Likewise, many guns rarely see the light of day beyond a nightstand, glove box, or closet, and most handguns, bought for purposes of self-protection, are never pointed at a human being. With regard to the larger problem of gun violence, none of this matters much, according to Schwarz. What matters, he argues, is that handguns are everywhere. No matter where one lives—in the city, in the suburbs, or in the country—if one household does not have a handgun, chances are another one nearby does, and it is the sheer number of, and easy access to, these weapons that adds to their lethality.[31]

Other social scientists similarly highlight the volume of guns as a singular problem. Joseph Sheley and James Wright, both sociologists at Tulane University and the authors of *In the Line of Fire: Youth, Guns, and Violence in Urban America* (1995), have explored those parts of the inner city where guns have become normative, and where young people perceive a need to carry and use firearms. Some of their findings are not surprising, while some are. For example, they find gun violence to be an overwhelmingly male and urban phenomenon; however, they also identify a kind of suburban arms race. "No longer can we portray juvenile firearm activity, at least exclusively, as a reflection of urban poverty," they report.[32] They also find correlations between guns, gangs, and drug usage, but the correlations are not as strong as one might imagine, and they find only limited correlation between peer influence, "respect," and gun usage. And while it is perhaps not surprising that many urban youth choose to arm themselves for self-protection, it is jarring to consider that many young criminals carry guns because of the possibility that their victims might be armed.

Sheley and Wright remind the reader that most of the methods used by juveniles to obtain guns are already against the law. For example, it is illegal for juveniles to purchase handguns through normal consumer channels: retail sale of handguns to anyone under the age of twenty-one and of rifles and shotguns to anyone under the age of eighteen is prohibited. Similarly, what some juveniles do with their guns is already illegal too: bringing a gun onto school property is unlawful in most jurisdictions. Many of the restrictions on youth apply to adults as well. It is illegal to cross state lines to purchase guns. Theft of guns from homes, cars, and shipments is illegal; transferring or selling stolen property is also illegal. Transferring a firearm to a person with a criminal record is illegal, as is possession of a gun by anyone with a history of alcohol or drug abuse. Unlicensed carrying of firearms is illegal everywhere, and discharging firearms within city limits is illegal almost everywhere. Assaults, robbery, murder, and other acts of violence are unlawful in every jurisdiction.

Gun controls at the point of sale, while essential, have limited effectiveness. The Brady Law, which established a national five-day waiting period for handgun purchases, cannot directly affect illicit commerce involving informal buys, swaps, and trades, and control of gun distribution at the retail level "seems not to fit the problem," according to Sheley and Wright, who contend that there is little that juveniles can now do within the law to obtain and carry guns.[33] Young people get firearms from friends, from family members, from the black market, and perhaps most important, from theft. "It is fairly obvious that theft is the ultimate (if not proximate) source of many or most of the firearms that now circulate in the informal street market," they write. Such theft, from their perspective, "erodes the distinction between legitimate and illegitimate firearms" (or between "right hands" and "wrong hands") because any firearm that can be possessed legally and legitimately can be stolen "and thus enter the illicit street commerce in guns." While Sheley and Wright's argument might seem to point to an absolute ban on firearms, it is not their intent to suggest as much. They point out that halting domestic production or confiscating guns would do little to prevent the manufacture of guns elsewhere in the world or their illegal importation into this country. "If it is possible to organize a system of commerce to bring hundreds of tons of cocaine from Colombia and get it into the hands of people on the streets of our cities, it is certainly possible to organize a system that will bring hundreds of tons of small arms from Israel or Switzerland or the Czech Republic or Brazil and supply a street market in firearms as well."[34]

What then can be done to address the problem? Having dismissed confiscation, reduced production, and further legislation, Sheley and Wright ultimately recommend finding a way to eradicate the need to carry guns, as opposed to eradicating guns themselves. "We can seek to impose our will, pass new legislation to outlaw that of which we disapprove, and insist on harsher punishments for those who defy our rules," they write. "Ultimately, however, convincing inner-city juveniles (or adults) not to own, carry, and use guns requires convincing them that they can survive in their neighborhoods without being armed, that they can come and go in peace, that their unarmed condition will not cause them to be victimized, intimidated, or slain."[35]

Sheley and Wright allude to the secret lives of guns, apart from the watchful eye of their owners. What happens when a gun is left unattended? Usually nothing. Most often they sit neglected, quietly rusting in a nightstand or propped in the corner of a closet. Sometimes, however, bad things happen, such as accidental shootings and theft. Government statistics reveal the scope of the latter problem. The "stolen gun file" at the FBI's National Crime Information Center contains more than two million reports, of which 60 percent are reports of stolen handguns. The Bureau of Justice Statistics, the number-crunching division of the Justice Department, estimates 340,000 incidents of firearm theft from private citizens each year from 1987 to 1992, or 1.7 million stolen guns in five years; more than half (53 percent) were handguns. The 1991 Survey of State Prison Inmates found that violent inmates were more likely to use a handgun than any other weapon (presumably before they were incarcerated), and that many adult and juvenile offenders had either stolen a firearm or kept, sold, or traded a stolen firearm.[36] The outcome of gun theft is inevitably a society with more guns in the hands of those who would do harm with them.

Handguns, like laptop computers, have legs; that is, the portability they afford translates into a greater susceptibility to theft, and they tend to "disappear." Criminals get their guns via an illicit gun market, supplied through theft from rightful owners who are usually law-abiding citizens; this theft blurs any useful distinction between legitimate and illegitimate guns. Efforts to stanch the flow of illegal guns while leaving law-abiding gun owners unscathed are therefore pointless. As long as anyone can own a firearm, criminals will own them too, and unless every gun is secured under lock and key, accidental shootings and theft will occur.

Firefight

Most arguments against gun control advocate keeping guns "out of the wrong hands": that is, preventing criminals from keeping and using firearms. The logic is that most gun owners are law-abiding citizens, and that most guns are used for legitimate purposes, not for the commission of a crime. The NRA slogan "Guns Don't Kill People, People Kill People" works from the premise that guns are inanimate objects, and that only human intent can animate them toward foul purposes. Why restrict law-abiding citizens when criminals are the ones using guns improperly? "Out of the wrong hands" also suggests keeping guns away from children, who might use them dangerously and irresponsibly.

Arguments against gun control avoid any clear links between the number of guns and gun violence, and instead emphasize the instances in which homeowners and business owners deterred crime by using a gun. They further emphasize that innocent, law-abiding citizens need protection, especially when the government and police cannot protect them. Gun control punishes only those who abide by the law, not criminals;

such arguments therefore emphasize "criminal control," not gun control. Greater policing, more prisons, and tougher sentencing address the real problem. Finally, they emphasize that the U.S. Constitution guarantees the individual right to bear arms.

Arguments for gun control, conversely, maintain that the Second Amendment does *not* imply the right of every citizen to own a gun. Instead, they maintain that the authors of the Bill of Rights, fearing a standing army, ensured a state's right to protect itself by forming a "well regulated militia," as is clearly mentioned in the text; accordingly, the right to bear arms was designed for states, not private citizens. Pointing to accidental deaths, thefts, and incidents in which guns are turned against those who own them, they show how guns victimize even their rightful owners. More prisons, increased sentences, and additional police are not a substitute for effective regulation; besides, these measures come too late for the victims of gun violence. These counterarguments often let the numbers of gun deaths speak for themselves.

There are several problems with the debate over guns, several assumptions that polarize the issue and stymie any real progress in addressing the larger problem of gun violence. None of them is peculiar to either pro-gun or anti-gun advocates; both sides routinely subscribe to these assumptions. The first is that the nation is populated with bad and good people: aggressive criminals who would use guns offensively and gun-packing citizens who would use guns defensively. The second is that guns are mere props, subjects of debate, rather than actors themselves in a larger drama of violence. The third is that the Constitution of the United States somehow holds the key to solving the question of gun control.

John Lott, author of *More Guns, Less Crime: Understanding Crime and Gun Control Laws* (1998), provides an opportunity to discuss this first assumption. Lott, an economist, argues quite simply that armed citizens stop crimes: the more armed citizens, the lower the rate of violent crime.[37] Intuition suggests that the exact opposite is true, but what of the possibilities that many of Lott's "armed citizens" may, in fact, be criminals, or that many otherwise law-abiding citizens will find trouble (or trouble will find them) if armed? Claiming to carry a gun for self-protection does not preclude malevolence, violent intent, or even criminal behavior. A burglar might honestly claim to carry a gun for self-protection, even though he is committing a crime and "defending himself" against a frightened homeowner wielding a gun; likewise, a marital quarrel can have an ugly ending if both parties know that there is a loaded pistol "to protect against burglars" in the nightstand. If Lott is correct about armed citizens and crime rates, then he is surely mistaken about armed citizens and gun violence: more armed citizens also means more accidental shootings, more thefts, and an aggregate jump in gun violence.

Joyce Lee Malcolm, author of *Guns and Violence: The English Experience* (2002), is Lott's British counterpart, making roughly the same argument. Looking at crime rates in England before modern restrictions, she finds that violent crime was rare when Brits were armed to the teeth; violent crime has skyrocketed now that they are disarmed. Like Lott, Malcolm concludes that guns reduce crime, and like him, she may be correct, but her starting assumption is comparably flawed. While a society awash in firearms may have lower crime rates, a reduction in crime is not the same as a reduction in violence. To argue that guns reduce violence is preposterous. Malcolm concludes her book by writing that "allowing individuals the means to protect themselves and also thereby to deter crime is not without some potential cost to the general quiet," effectively equating the tens of thousands of people killed by firearms each year with the broken eggs needed to make an omelet.[38]

As evidenced by Lott's and Malcolm's arguments, much of the debate over guns presumes that the nation is populated with good guys and bad guys, armed citizens versus criminals. In reality, the lines are much more fluid. How does one account for the numerous deaths—accidental and otherwise—at the hands of "good citizens"? While exact numbers vary, statistics show that a gun is more likely to be used against a family member than against an intruder.[39] To reduce this counterpoint to its simplest terms: guns sometimes lead good people to do bad things. And what of bad people doing good things? Such arguments presume a criminal element so predatory that it obeys no laws, but, of course, most criminals are only criminals part-time, going about their daily business the rest of the time like everyone else. Most of what they do on any given day is done in accord with the law and with societal expectations. How does one arm the good guys while disarming the bad guys? Waiting until the bad guys have differentiated themselves by committing a violent crime does nothing to reduce levels of violence. It only addresses the problem after the fact.

The second assumption hinges on the neutrality of guns, on guns as inanimate hunks of steel. Gun control advocates who have singled out certain guns as undesirable know this assumption well. In the 1970s, critics focused on "Saturday Night Specials": small, cheap, poorly manufactured, often imported handguns, criticized as having no legitimate purpose and seemingly preferred by criminals. In the 1980s, the National Coalition to Ban Handguns and Handgun Control Inc. condemned all handguns in general, and in the 1990s, politicians singled out so-called assault weapons (semiautomatic rifles with military trappings) as worthy of regulatory legislation. Critics on both sides of the debate pointed out why such characterizations were doomed to fail (even if the desired legislation was passed).[40] First, guns themselves are neither good nor bad. Usage follows the intent of the handler. Second, any gun can be utilized for something other than its intended purpose. A target gun, for example, can be employed for self-defense, just as a paramilitary weapon can be used to hunt. Therefore, it is assumed, guns are neutral.

There is a certain Zen-like logic to this perspective. When given an opportunity, a gun will do what it is intended to do, which is punch holes: in hillsides and creek banks, paper targets and tin cans, birds and animals, people, and anything else at which it is fired, intentionally or not. Bullets are similarly brainless, nothing more than missiles seeking targets. Such a perspective considers guns to be utilitarian objects and renders the destruction caused by them (and any judgment of this destruction) incidental.

But what if the mere presence of guns creates a situation in which escalated violence can occur? Regardless of the intent of the handler, guns may be seen as catalysts for violence, not only permitting violence but stimulating it too. Leonard Berkowitz has noted that the finger pulls the trigger, "but the trigger may also be pulling the finger." As one young gangster has explained, a gun "wants to get blood on itself. . . . It want to get a body on it." It comes as little surprise that in a heavily armed society people have found it wise to shoot first and ask questions later. Some scholars have found evidence of guns as "aggression-eliciting stimuli," others have not; but if guns "want" to be used then their neutrality might be questioned. Just as the misapplication of "noncriminal" guns is troubling, so too is the relatively unexplored idea that guns themselves cause violence.[41]

The third assumption explains why constitutional schol-ars and policy makers alike try to divine the original intent of the Founding Fathers. The "illusion of power and choice" de-scribed by Garret Keizer speaks to the threat of government confiscation, which ranks high among the fears of some gun enthusiasts and informs the massive resistance to any kind of reasonable gun control. From this perspective, gun control is a slippery slope in which any restriction represents another step toward the eventual confiscation of all privately owned guns. Part of this worry stems from the ongoing constitutional debate over firearms: in such an environment, any piece of anti-gun legislation constitutes a basis for legal challenge of the Second Amendment to anyone already sensitized to his or her seem-ingly imperiled right to own a gun. The resulting paranoia over confiscation forms the cornerstone of NRA mobilization against gun control. Many gun magazines and online blogs would lead one to believe that government confiscation of firearms is nigh, as do the words of NRA president Charlton Heston, who in 1997 told the National Press Club in Washington, D.C., "We are again engaged in a great civil war—a cultural war that's about to hijack you right out of your own birthright."[42] Such beliefs have given rise to shrill proclamations such as, "You can have my gun when you pry it from my cold dead fingers," popular-ized on bumper stickers in the 1980s.

In far right circles, confiscation inevitably draws compari-sons to Hitler's Third Reich, and although some gun owners perceive a threat to their gun caches, the chances of gun confis-cation by the federal government are practically nil. While cer-tain states and cities have stricter gun control laws than oth-ers, no systematic efforts have been made at the national level to confiscate firearms in private possession. "The Day When All the Guns Are Gathered Up—what the paranoids regard as the end of the world and the Pollyannas as the Rapture—it's never going to happen," writes Garret Keizer. "All of this is so much fantasy, another example of the disingenuousness that tends to color our discussion of guns."[43] One could further add that the proliferation of guns in American society renders the academic debate over the Second Amendment and the origins of private gun ownership rather moot: if possession is nine-tenths of the law, then the discussion over the constitutionality of the right to bear arms is nine-tenths settled.

There are, however, other ways of looking at gun violence and gun control that reframe the issue—not in terms of right or wrong hands, or proper and improper usage, but instead in terms of the functionality (or instrumentality) of guns and the sheer number of firearms in the United States. There are also measures that have not been fully explored that would allow law-abiding citizens to continue to enjoy shooting sports while reducing levels of gun violence. Such solutions require not only rationality but also a recognition that reasonable gun control is an initial, intermediate step in reducing gun violence, not the final solution in destroying American liberty, as some gun enthusiasts fear; as such it is *not* a radical measure but in fact a very modest one, intended to strengthen existing liberties, to preserve the status quo, and to better quality of life. In other words, gun control is a conservative response to a very liberal gun policy. What may be necessary, however, is a wholesale shift in American values: a move away from a gun veneration that encourages not only gun ownership but also the use of firearms to shoot people.

Click, Click, Boom

Most individuals probably reside neither in the pro-control or anti-control camp, for reasons that are clear. "'Do you support gun control?' constitutes a question so imprecise as to be almost meaningless," argues William Vizzard, professor of criminal justice at Cal State–Sacramento and former ATF agent. "The question presumes a world composed of two discreet classes of people: those who favor guns and oppose all gun control, and those who detest guns and seek their prohibition." Don Kates agrees, noting that the majority of Americans, including a majority of gun owners, favor a stance that recognizes "a need to accommodate legitimate gun owner interests" while understanding "the social imperative for controlling a dangerous instrumentality."[44]

The arguments about guns and gun control in the United States are as tired as those regarding media violence. While studio executives and parental watchdogs have succeeded in maintaining a debate about an issue that could have and should have been resolved years ago, the gun nuts and gun grabbers alike have perpetuated an even longer argument, worn in its aphorisms. It is a debate controlled at the fringes: at one extreme are those who would ban all guns, and at the other are those who would increase the armament of our already heavily armed nation. Gary Kleck, professor of criminology at Florida State University, has characterized this debate as a "dialogue of the deaf."[45] What is needed are fresh perspectives and ways of avoiding the dichotomous talking points that inevitably lead to retrenchment and stalemate.

One fairly new and interesting perspective is brought to bear by public health professionals who approach gun violence from outside the debate over gun control. For example, in *Gun Violence: The Real Costs* (2000), Philip Cook and Jens Ludwig calculate an actual dollar amount for the annual costs of gun violence in the United States: $100 billion in medical treatments, lost earnings, and the like. Acknowledging that such figures are a poor measure of the real burden that gun violence imposes on society, they argue that gun violence reduces the quality of life for everyone in the United States:

> In short, most all of us bear some part of the costs of gun violence, in myriad ways: waiting in line to pass through airport security; buying a transparent book bag for school-aged children to meet their school's post-Columbine regulations; paying taxes for the protection of public officials, for urban renewal projects in areas devastated by gun violence, for subsidizing an urban trauma center; living in fear that one's children may be injured by a stray bullet or that a despon-

dent relative would get her hands on a gun. And no one is entirely safe from becoming a victim themselves.[46]

Fewer guns equal less harm, they conclude, noting, "The evidence to the contrary, no matter how often repeated and with what vehemence, does not stand up to close scrutiny."[47]

David Hemenway—professor of public health at Harvard University, director of Harvard's Injury Control Research Center and Youth Violence Prevention Center, and author of *Private Guns, Public Health* (2004)—adopts a similar approach to gun violence, which he calls "a modern-day public health epidemic":

> The public health approach is not interested in blaming anything or anyone but instead looks to prevent. The public health approach broadens the policy options from an exclusive focus on holding individual citizens responsible for their actions (which they should be) to also considering ways to improve the physical and social environment (1) to reduce the likelihood of impulsive, imprudent, improper, and immoral behavior and (2) to reduce the harm done by such conduct.[48]

Approaching gun violence as a public health issue as Cook, Ludwig, and Hemenway do provides a new angle on the debate over gun control—not because the public health perspective is apolitical or free from bias but because it rests on notions of community and shared fate. "Public health professionals seek only to reduce injuries and death," Hemenway writes. "Promoting reasonable gun policies does not make them 'anti-gun' any more than the Insurance Institute for Highway Safety is 'anti-car.'"[49]

It is all too easy to view gun violence as someone else's problem, but as Cook and Ludwig observe, "The public concern about gun violence has much to do with the safety of loved ones, neighbors, classmates, members of the same church or temple, public figures, and others who have enough of a personal connection that their death or injury would have emotional impact."[50] Mutual concern not only enhances the value of creating a safer community but also serves as a foundation for any meaningful reduction in gun violence. Whatever progress is to be made in reducing gun violence lies in the recognition that every "loose" gun—whether unlocked, unsupervised, unnumbered, or unregistered—poses a threat to every single citizen. When enough of us feel the threat to ourselves and to our loved ones, then the scales may tip toward public policy change and responsible civic action; until then, the debate over guns and gun control will be steered by those at its extremes.

Guns can serve positive functions, not the least of which is providing a sense of security. However, the peace of mind afforded by a gun comes at a steep price. If that peace of mind could be achieved some other way, then surely that possibility would be worth exploring.

CHAPTER 4

Red, Black, and Blue

"... a malenky bit of ultraviolence ..."
—Anthony Burgess, *A Clockwork Orange*
(1963)

Are You Not Entertained?

The epic film *Gladiator* (2000) explores not only human beings' appetite for destruction but also the capacity of "civilized" societies for violence, and in exploring the barbarity of ancient Rome the film neatly satirizes the modern United States and its own fascination with violent entertainment. In the beginning, the fearless Roman general Maximus is renowned for his bravery and loyalty to the Roman emperor, Marcus Aurelius. After years of fighting for Rome, Maximus is betrayed by his beloved Caesar's son, Commodus. When his wife and son are brutally murdered, the general is enslaved and forced to become a gladiator. At first he resists the degraded savagery of gladiatorial combat; later, a new sponsor encourages the ex-soldier to achieve greatness by wooing and winning the crowd. In the end, Maximus avenges his family, destroys the evil emperor, and achieves peace.

The film's protagonist and antagonist represent two different embodiments of not only manhood but also the role of violence in entertainment: the valiant gladiator Maximus, struggling for survival in front of the Coliseum crowd, versus the treacherous villain Commodus, Rome's Caesar whose embrace of barbarism eventually destroys him. The relationship between the violence, the crowd, and the hero develops throughout the film, beginning with the opening battle scene, which serves to establish Maximus as a hero. The violence serves its primary purpose and the audience is entertained. The Roman emperor is similarly established: it is clear from the first meeting with Commodus, who arrives after the opening battle has ended, that he is a weak, cowardly man because he does not fight. He shirks away from real violence but develops a love of violent entertainment, in the form of mock skirmishes, war games, and gladiatorial combat. He is incompetent, boyish, cowardly. The emperor, who is aware of weakness and his fear of confrontation, seeks validation elsewhere; out of this need arises Commodus the gladiator fanatic, the original sports fan. The film suggests that participating in violence confirms manhood, while watching it emasculates the spectator, but Commodus's fascination with brutality as sport molds him into a reckless and dangerous leader who jeopardizes Roman hegemony. Rather than focusing on just rule and the principles of democracy, Commodus selfishly focuses on his own bloodlust, relying also on his people's prurient interest in violent spectacle. Director Ridley Scott holds up a mirror to the viewers, inviting them to see in Commodus their own fascination with violent entertainment.

Maximus must learn to kill more theatrically. When he first enters the arena, his matter-of-fact, efficient, and realistic approach to combat does not appeal to his audience. He slaughters his opponents, throws down his sword, and spits in the dust, shouting to the audience, "Are you not entertained?" Confronted with the reality of bloodshed, or perhaps already desensitized to it, the audience sits in numbed silence. Maximus, initially disgusted by the combat, changes his act to win the crowd. He learns to build tension, create suspense, and supersede his own levels of violence—much like the modern entertainment industry—and the audience keeps pace. Commodus, the modern audience member, sits in his throne, watching. With each innovation in killing, his enjoyment and satisfaction decreases. Inured to violence, Commodus—who avoids violence for most of the film—is no longer satisfied to simply watch: to slake his thirst for blood, he must now participate.

In the end, Maximus, the reluctant entertainer, and Commodus, the reluctant combatant, square off in the arena. Commodus cheats, camouflaging Maximus's stab wound to perpetuate the illusion of reality for the enjoyment of his audience.

Commodus becomes the valiant gladiator, facing his opponent in all-too-real mock combat; Maximus relinquishes his role as gladiator to face his opponent as a true enemy, not as one to be slain for the enjoyment of the crowd. Commodus, lost in his own fantastic delusions, believes he is entering a make-believe world in which he controls the outcomes: he fails to understand that the fiction he has created is in fact now reality. Maximus ultimately slays Commodus, but dies afterward as a result of Commodus's *ob scena* attack. Reality consumes entertainment as entertainment consumes reality. The film suggests that if violence is tolerated and in fact nurtured in an otherwise civil society, then the line between entertainment and reality will eventually distort to the point of obfuscation: in effect, the line ceases to exist.

Gladiator hints that the United States is not so far removed from ancient Rome. Like the Romans, Americans have created a society unparalleled in its achievements and cultural production, and if the Roman empire could fall as a result of seeking pleasure in mayhem, then so too could the American empire. When the Visigoths sacked Rome in 410, the Romans thought it was the end of civilization. In a way it was, of course, as an empire crumbled to technological impoverishment and comparative backwardness—but it was moral bankruptcy, as much as anything, that toppled Rome from the inside out.

What have we to learn from the ancient Romans? Does our nation face a similar crisis, brought about by a comparable fascination not only with violence but also with excess? As Gavin de Becker writes in his best-selling book *The Gift of Fear: Survival Signals That Protect Us from Violence* (1997),

> In a very real sense, the surging water in an ocean does not move; rather, energy moves through it. In this same sense, the energy of violence moves through our culture. Some experience it as a light but unpleasant breeze, easy to tolerate. Others are destroyed by it, as if by a hurricane. But nobody—nobody—is untouched. Violence is a part of America. . . . It is around us, and it is in us. As the most powerful people in history, we have climbed to the top of the world food chain, so to speak. Facing not one single enemy or predator who poses

> to us any danger of consequence, we've found the only prey left: ourselves.[1]

If the United States has begun to cannibalize itself in self-directed paroxysms of rage as ancient Rome once did, then we may only hope to apprehend—before the point of no return—a truth that the Romans never acknowledged in their exploration of violence for its own sake: how we entertain ourselves matters.

Imagining Dystopia

It is no stretch to see the kindred bloodlust of the Coliseum spectators in our own enthusiasm for rough sports, and those who seek them will note other parallels between ancient Rome and the modern American empire. Like Rome, the United States has achieved a global empire; like Rome, the United States has found it a mixed blessing; like Rome, the United States is fascinated by and consumed with violence; and like the Romans, Americans crave a violent realism in entertainment that threatens to rend civil society. Although the United States has perhaps not attained Rome's heights—or matched its lows—certainly we have cultivated a similar bloodlust, and if U.S. civilization is following a similar declension narrative, then we do it not unknowingly. Violence in our media is a form of dangerous hyperbole. It is not new—only bolder, larger, and more pervasive that it once was.

It is this exaggerated sense of American violence that has led Hollywood to proffer futuristic visions of a nation corrupted by its fascination with violent sport. Over the past several decades, various films have imagined dystopia forged in spectacle and bloodlust. For example, *Rollerball* (1975), the more comedic and satirical *Death Race 2000* (1978), and *The Running Man* (1987) all deal with the popularity of death sport in sci-fi fantasy futures. Starring James Caan, the big-budget *Rollerball* depicts the ritualization of violence in a kind of high-speed, high-stakes roller derby. By presenting the competitors as gladiators struggling to maintain individuality in a totalitarian regime that would consume them, the film paradoxically succeeds in glamorizing what it also condemns. In *Death Race 2000*, a low-budget appropriation of *Rollerball*, cross-country auto racers are the national heroes. By the year 2000, the citizenry of the United Provinces of America, emotionally dulled by the Great Depression of 1979 and unceasing wars with other nations, thrill only to the violence of the Transcontinental Road Race, in which drivers score points by running down pedestrians in a mad, coast-to-coast rush—with bonus points awarded for killing women, children, the elderly, and the handicapped. A creation of Roger Corman's New World Productions, *Death Race 2000* straddles the line between sleazy, grind-house exploitation and satire, redeemed less by the acting presences of David Carradine and Sylvester Stallone than by its smart commentary on audience participation in vicarious violence. In both *Rollerball* and *Death Race 2000*, corporate sponsors and political leaders use the athletes to bleed off, figuratively and literally, the discontent of the masses who find catharsis in the carnage. *The Running Man* taps a similar theme, seeming to anticipate the reality-television craze of the early twenty-first century in its pro-wrestling-style showmanship. Arnold Schwarzenegger stars as an ex-cop framed for a terrible crime he did not commit. Sentenced to serve on the game show The Running Man, he must evade comic-book killers with names like Buzzsaw and SubZero as he navigates an urban maze toward prizes and freedom.

If these films anticipate a future in which violence for its own sake occupies the cultural center, then that future may already exist. It is possible to ignore the rawest of the raw—the most acute, immoderate, and excessive kinds of violence—so long as they exist on the periphery and so long as social mores define them as extreme. But what happens when the extreme becomes increasingly ordinary? Mainstreaming extreme violence is problematic because that violence becomes normalized and habitual in daily American life. Once normalization occurs it is difficult to gain critical perspective on the violence, making it part of the warp and woof of everyday life.

Perhaps these fears are the same that haunt every generation. From the earliest days of American cinema, someone has always bemoaned the brutal violence, the depiction of antisocial behaviors, the immoderate sexual content. Often these critics have been moral absolutists offering a pious critique of what they perceive to be the laxity of an increasingly secular society. For these viewers the flash of a woman's breast or the sympathetic portrayal of a thief represents an on-screen threat as reprehensible as any rape or vicious killing. Their concerns, while not irrelevant, are not the primary concern with regard to mainstreaming violence; anything short of what they define as "wholesome" entertainment will fall short of the mark. The bigger concern is that tolerance of violence is expanding as depictions of violence become more pervasive and—importantly—that a majority of people has become insulated to the violability of humanity that violence represents.

The Combat Culture

Few phenomena illustrate this concern like the combat culture that has grown steadily and organically across the United States since the 1990s: a culture of brawling that includes both professional and amateur fights, organized and unorganized, formal and informal. Fighters are young and old; generally male; sometimes trained, often not. The combat culture often involves a kind of extreme, ungloved boxing with few if any rules. At one end of the spectrum are professional fighters who clash in public spectacles reminiscent of gladiatorial combat; at the other end are armies of amateur pugilists whose reasons for fighting range from blind rage to mere boredom.

Professionally trained fighters participate in mixed martial arts (MMA) competitions such as the Ultimate Fighting Championship (UFC), whose original aim was to pit combatants from different disciplines against one another. Who would win in a fight: a boxer or someone who practices judo? A wrestler or a karate master? MMA would presumably settle such theoretical questions. Over the past ten years, MMA has emerged as a hybridized sport with its own rules of bushido, drawing heavily on boxing and jiu-jitsu. Mixed martial artists are highly trained, highly conditioned, and highly brutal athletes. Combatants fight until stopped by the referee; there is no standing eight count. Stoppages occur when one fighter is down and unconscious or when one is choked out or forced into submission with grappling techniques. A fighter aims for a knockout, throwing hands even after bringing an opponent to his knees, pummeling the opponent on the ground until the referee mercifully steps in to stop the reign of blows. Victory is assured when one "mounts" an opponent by straddling his torso and pounding him like a schoolyard bully. Fighters train to punch a prone opponent by pounding a punching bag on the mat.

The rise of UFC in the late 1990s and early 2000s was swift and unexpected, the latest in a trend toward more extreme versions of familiar sports; however, unlike these other fads, UFC has moved quickly into mainstream culture alongside other long-established sports "in a way that goes well beyond fleeting trend," according to L. Jon Wertheim, *Sports Illustrated* writer and author of *Blood in the Cage* (2009).[2] The money and numbers involved have been impressive. *The Ultimate Fighter*, the UFC's weekly reality show on Spike TV, often eclipses the television ratings of the NBA and baseball playoffs among the target audience, the eighteen-to-thirty-four male demographic. On pay-per-view, UFC outperforms boxing and pro-wrestling. According to Wertheim, UFC's 2006 pay-per-view revenues were nearly $223 million, compared with $177 million for boxing and $200 million for World Wrestling Entertainment (WWE). In May 2007, the sixty-ninth card of the UFC's bloody existence—"UFC 69: Shootout" in Houston—was the highest grossing event in the history of the Toyota Center; the second highest was a Rolling Stones concert in 2005.[3]

Pat Miletich, a highly successful MMA coach and a decorated fighter himself, explains the sport's popularity: "It seems like there are fewer and fewer opportunities to find out who you really are. With this combination of violence and discipline—brains and brawn—you have a hell of a way to find out. Same thing from the fan's perspective. There's no b.s. Two guys are stripped down. One wins, one loses. Where else do you get that anymore?"[4] He sounds not unlike Tyler Durden, the protagonist in Chuck Palahniuk's novel *Fight Club* (1996) who establishes an underground, bare-knuckle, boxing club to recapture some sense of being alive in a materialist, consumer-oriented world; members pledged to silence ("You don't talk of Justice reports that males consistently experience higher victimization rates than females for all types of violent crime except rape and sexual assault. Private gun ownership in the United States runs four times higher among men than women despite industry efforts to increase female gun ownership.[1]

While most men never kill, rape, or even commit assault, it is clear that most violent acts occur at the hands of men. It is also clear that societal norms sometimes begrudgingly respect the attitudes and assumptions that lead to violent male expression. Therefore, understanding the characteristics of masculinity that lead to male aggression, violence, or criminal behavior provides a good starting point for any discussion of violence.

Cowboys and Indians

Why do men behave violently? Is violence biologically determined? Or is it culturally determined—in other words, is violence somehow related to "American-ness," or what it means to be American? David T. Courtwright offers one explanation in his book *Violent Land: Single Men and Social Disorder from the Frontier to the Inner City* (1996). "Increased libido, impulsiveness, and aggressiveness" caused by high testosterone levels, and the common loss of "physical capacity and sexual drive" with aging, helps to explain why young men are biologically predetermined to act violently, according to the author.[2] Working from this assumption, Courtwright argues that "insofar as young, single men are any society's most troublesome and unruly citizens, America had a built-in tendency toward violence and disorder."[3] His premise rests on a simple syllogism: young men are predisposed to act aggressively, and the nineteenth-century American frontier had lots of single young men; ergo, there was a lot of violence on the American frontier.

"This book is not—and no study of violence should be—a reductive exercise in historical sociobiology," assures Courtwright, who takes pains to show that a mix of demographic, cultural, and social factors amplified whatever violent tendencies young men naturally carried into the American West. The infamous Dodge City, Kansas—with its overabundance of buf-

CHAPTER 1

The Violence of American Masculinity

> Men are rewarded for learning the
> practice of violence in virtually any
> sphere of activity by money, admiration,
> recognition, respect, and the genuflection
> of others honoring their sacred and
> proven masculinity.
> —Andrea Dworkin, *Pornography* (1979)

Boys Will Be Boys

The first step in thinking violence is to recognize it as a largely male phenomenon. While women are increasingly committing violent acts, casual observation confirms that men commit more than women and that they aggress more often—not only against women but also against other men. Men top all major crime indexes; it is men who fill prisons. Domestic violence is overwhelmingly committed by husbands against wives; criminal rape, which shades into sexual intercourse under pressure, is also overwhelmingly committed by men. Men fight more often, participating in body-contact sports such as boxing and football that involve ritualized combat and injury. The thirty million soldiers who compose the world's fighting forces are overwhelmingly men (and in some countries only men). It is men who almost exclusively make the decisions that lead to armed conflict and war.

Statistics confirm what we already know about this gendered aspect of violence. The United States ranks first among industrialized nations in violent death rates, and men are most frequently the assailants and the victims, according to the U.S. Department of Health and Human Services. The Bureau unavoidable, human. Viewing it can be cathartic, offering a steam valve that averts real-life violence. It is a legitimate source of entertainment; it is exciting, fun to watch, and harmless. News and entertainment media only reflect what violence already exists in the world. Guns, while sometimes destructive, are a constitutionally protected freedom and an integral part of our American heritage. Other than lock up criminals when they break the law, there is not much we can do about violence because, as H. Rap Brown said in the 1960s, it is "as American as cherry pie."[25]

As long as such assumptions prevail, violence will continue to escalate and lessen the quality of life in the United States. Americans lack a certain *viosense*, or heightened awareness of the ways in which violence manifests itself in society, and if we want to make progress in combating violence, broadly defined, then we must first adjust our perspectives on it. We must reposition it from the monotonous humdrum of daily existence to the foreground of consciousness, listening carefully to what has essentially become white noise. We must recapture outrage in knowing that such life-defying events happen in our midst with stunning regularity. We must open our eyes to what is happening and attempt to understand.[26]

We must also consider violence anew, with open minds. We must look at the data, critically and unflinchingly, and acknowledge that conventional wisdom is often wrong. At the same time, we must recognize that so-called experts, from criminologists to psychologists, sometimes use informational monopolies to serve their own ends, and we must be willing to cut through the confusing thicket of research findings with common sense and reason. We must steel ourselves to confront disturbing subject matter. In order to lessen the effects of violence, we must first address a host of interrelated issues, untangling them as we look for correlations and unanticipated connections; and, in order to do that, we must first reconsider our assumptions, recondition our minds, and redirect our thoughts.

In short, we must cultivate viosense. We must think violence.

lem that ranges from obscene hand gestures and tailgating to violent confrontations ending in death. The U.S. Department of Transportation estimates that two-thirds of traffic fatalities between 1990 and 1996 were at least partially attributable to aggressive driving. A study by the American Automotive Association (AAA) Foundation for Traffic Safety recorded 10,037 incidents of aggressive driving, including 218 deaths, during the same period. The problem of rage is not just limited to driving. About 5 percent of Americans have such frequent and serious blowups that they qualify as suffering from a new psychiatric diagnosis that mimics the parlance of the war in Iraq: IED, or Intermittent Explosive Disorder.[24]

Road rage, homeless bashing, and IED are the newest in a list of violent behaviors that have demanded public attention over the past several decades; considered together, these individual malignities constitute a larger culture of violence. Crime in the 1960s, gangs in the 1970s, drive-by shootings in the 1980s, carjackings in the 1990s—each has menaced the public imagination as the newest form of social dysfunction. And while addressing each in turn has met with limited success, addressing them all together has proven difficult. For whatever reason, tackling violence in general has seemed too great a challenge. Americans launched wars on drugs and, later, on terror, but there was no war on violence: we seemed to lack the ambition or the know-how or even the language to attack broad-spectrum violence. Instead, we settled in with it, made peace with it, and treated it as part of our cultural landscape, part of our heritage. Therefore, while individual problems have come and gone (or more accurately submerged and resurfaced), the larger culture of violence remains.

As violent incidents have become commonplace and everyday, so have our attitudes and beliefs regarding them softened; as our attitudes have softened, so have the incidents become commonplace and everyday. Accordingly, we have achieved a certain tolerance of violence that symbiotically joins with our assumptions about it, allowing us to function amid the carnage. We repeat platitudes that become shibboleths in the non-war against violence. After all, we tell ourselves, it is a violent world. People—especially men—are inherently violent. Whether interpersonal or international, violence is natural, about fight club") happily pummel one another as a test of manhood. Wertheim provides other reasons for MMA's popularity that supplement Miletich's almost primal explanation. Fans have been turned off by the corruption and mismanagement of boxing. MMA is more visceral, more in-your-face, more real. It is an all-American sport with little crossover appeal at a time when other sports are globalizing. And it is—almost impossibly—more violent than boxing.[5]

This latter point bears emphasis. Boxing worked hard to gain approbation as a legitimate sport by instituting safety rules; now it is viewed by MMA enthusiasts as tame and predictable. The irony of course is that boxing is not far removed from nineteenth-century bare-knuckle prizefighting, itself barely evolved from the no-holds-barred contests of the American frontier in which fighters stabbed and stomped one another, and gouged out each other's eyes. Today boxers still kill each other with some regularity in the ring: by one count there have been nearly nine hundred deaths from ring-sustained injuries since 1920. When boxing—a sport in which one outcome of proficiency is death—is the "safe," civilized standard by which we judge other combat sports, then the latter must be pretty rough indeed.[6]

Top-ranking MMA fighters earn six-figure sums per fight—seven figures if one counts bonuses, a percentage of pay-per-view sales, and endorsements—but many others fight for free. Those amateurs who swing away in imitation of their favorite MMA fighters enjoy a similar thrill of competition; the fights themselves have the same combination of striking and grappling, the same amount of blood, and the same tendency to end quickly in a knockout or submission. Courtesy of the Internet, the fights also have a similarly wide audience.[7]

The combat culture thrives online, where fighting has a visible presence, including many videos of kids fighting. Nothing new here—kids have always fought—but three things are remarkable in this regard. First, many of these fights have been captured on cell-phone cameras and similar devices, and many of them clearly have been staged, conducted expressly for the purpose of being filmed and posted online. To illustrate, in one video recorded at Southwind Middle School in Memphis, Tennessee, two girls fight in the locker room as other kids chant, "MySpace, MySpace," referring to the free online community and popular social networking website.[8] Second, under the auspices of instruction and "fighting tips," various websites post videos of school kids fighting at school, in parking lots, in backyards—anywhere and everywhere. So some people—including, presumably, many adults—are deriving enjoyment from seeing these videos. But third and finally, what is most remarkable in these video-captured events is the reaction of the spectators. Instead of pulling the combatants apart, crowds of spectators cheer them on, or sometimes stand by mutely to watch. The most troubling aspect of the fight videos posted on YouTube and similar websites is not the blood but rather the lack of intervention: onlookers simply circle and watch—sometimes tittering nervously, often quietly observing—as combatants punch and kick past the point of "winning" or submission. Like a professional MMA bout, the fight is not finished until one of the combatants is prone or unconscious; unlike the UFC, no referee monitors the action and there is no stoppage. No one interferes, even after one or the other has been knocked to the ground, unconscious. A thrashing can continue indefinitely: bystanders often fail to step in to prevent a mudholing or stomping.

YouTube, the popular online video site, boasts countless amateur fight videos, running the gamut from bar fights caught on tape to kids wrestling in the backyard. Again, nothing necessarily new here: one can witness drunken clashes on a Saturday night at watering holes in Anytown, USA, and playground scraps happen everyday. What is new is the titillation and addictive fascination of posting and viewing online videos of these encounters, and YouTube is a favorite forum for them. Because its video clips are not prescreened, YouTube's rules for posting content serve more like guidelines; a spokesman for the site told BBC News in July 2007 that prescreening content is a form of censorship beyond the purview of a private company. The site, owned by Google, does not allow the uploading of pornography, but violence is acceptable as long as it does not depict an actual incident of harm. Videos containing adult content are accessible to any visitor claiming to be at least eighteen years old. YouTube does not employ anyone to police what is posted on its website, relying instead on users to flag inappropriate films. When YouTube did change its policy the following year, it pledged to ban submissions that involve "inciting others to violence"; however, this change stemmed from complaints by Senator Joseph Lieberman, I-Connecticut, that the site was open to terrorist groups disseminating militant propaganda—not from any moral compunction about showing kids fighting. Still, hundreds of fight videos pop up.[9]

A cursory web search reveals a nationwide fascination with backyard brawls—everything from kids imitating pro-wrestlers to grown men slugging each other for money or just for kicks. In 2000 *Time* magazine reported on the high school boys of the Extreme Wrestling Federation in Sayreville, New Jersey; the Alliance of Violence in South Euclid, Ohio; and a group in Poinciana, Florida, called Insane Violent Hardcore Extreme Wrestling. Each of these amateur wrestling "federations" organized weekly bouts in which they wore costumes, created elaborate storylines, and bloodied one another with moves copied from their favorite pro-wrestlers—including whacking each other with folding metal chairs. More than four hundred leagues had websites and many traded homemade videotapes of their bouts. Injuries are common and fatalities do occur, the most infamous being the killing of six-year-old Tiffany Eunick by twelve-year-old Lionel Tate in Broward County, Florida, in 2001. Tate, convicted of first-degree murder, became the youngest person in the United States sentenced to life in prison.[10]

Perhaps not surprisingly, MMA has also caught on with children. In March 2008 the Associated Press reported that bare-knuckle fighting had caught on in Missouri, where fighters as young as six are encouraged by parents who "treat the sport as casually as wrestling, Little League, or soccer." While a few states have no regulations, many treat youth participation in formal MMA training as a misdemeanor; the article identified Missouri as "the only state in the nation that explicitly allows the youth fights." Still, the trend has been alarming to medical experts and sports officials worried about the breaking points of little bodies, and to parents worried about the message being sent.[11]

When kids imitate professional athletes, we should not be surprised by the accompanying nastiness. A certain brutality defines modern-day professional and semiprofessional sports.

Such is the climate of college football that Ryan Schmidt, an offensive lineman for the University of South Florida, can freely tell the *St. Petersburg Times*,

> I don't play dirty, but I definitely don't shy away from taking my shots on people. When I get my chance to hit someone when they're not looking or hit someone from behind, I'll take my shot. That's just how I've always played. My high school coach (in Boca Raton) was very adamant on taking shots at people that aren't looking. It's just playing hard. I don't think it's dirty in a sense. They'd do it to me if I wasn't looking.[12]

Coaches encourage such attitudes. "[Schmidt] is a gentleman off the field, but when he buckles on his chinstrap, he's going to play football and get the job done, whatever it takes," says USF coach Mike Simmonds, himself an NFL lineman for four seasons. "He's got a nasty disposition on the field. It's the way you're supposed to play the game."[13]

If sport is a metaphor for life, then the problem of sports violence—excessive violence on the field of play, goonism, dehumanizing one's opponent, lack of sportsmanship, playing with intent to harm—reveals something about the place of violence in American life. Professional and amateur sports alike harbor their own brand of brutal behaviors. On- and off-court brawls; fans celebrating their team's victory by destroying part of their own city; parents attacking coaches, referees, and each other for perceived injustices; a college team defending itself against charges of rape; and star athletes as steroid-enraged or gun-toting perpetrators of violent crime have all become part of the landscape of American sports. Not surprisingly, the brutality in sports informs everyday life, where it offers little in the way of catharsis. One need look no further for evidence of the synergistic nature of violent sport than NFL superstar Michael Vick, the quarterback for the Atlanta Falcons who, on August 20, 2007, accepted a plea offer from federal prosecutors in a criminal case stemming from a dog-fighting ring run from his Virginia farm. The inherent violence of professional football was apparently not enough for Vick, a former Virginia Tech standout who illegally pitted aggressive breeds against one another and who allegedly electrocuted, hanged, drowned, tortured, shot, and gruesomely killed those dogs that did not fight to his expectations. Vick served nineteen months before being released from prison to home confinement on May 20, 2009. As of September 2009, he was once again playing professional football as a backup quarterback for the Philadelphia Eagles.[14]

Desensitization and Ratings Creep

Michael Vick serves as a cautionary tale: a superlative athlete achieving the pinnacle of legitimate sport, only to plunge into criminal vice. His brand of amusement has found a niche in the deepest recesses of cyberspace: the shadowy realm of killing sports such as cockfighting, dogfighting, bullfighting, and animal baiting. Plumbing the darker depths of the Internet—at once the most extraordinary encyclopedia of human knowledge and the most sordid repository of humankind's darkest fascinations—allows one access to lurid entertainments such as violent pornography and so-called bumfights, in which videographers pay homeless men to spar.[15] Few would disagree that such pursuits represent a special depravity, but the existence of these entertainments is perhaps less troublesome than how we are likely to respond to them, given their contextualization and juxtaposition alongside backyard brawls and MMA contests. Indeed, the dangers of immersion in the combat culture parallel the dangers of habitual consumption of ultraviolent media content; if media violence renders one unable to distinguish the pain and suffering of real violence from the staged violence of movies and television, then the combat culture enables one to take pleasure in another's pain. Both, in desensitizing and habituating the viewer/participant to brutality, reinforce one another in facilitating a failure to understand the potential of violence for negative outcomes.

The dangers of habituating people to violence and brutality through the pervasive and fashionable aesthetic of violence for its own sake should be self-evident. As one scholar has cautioned, in aestheticizing violence "we can invoke the beauty of the presentation and thus be absolved from condemning ourselves for poor taste."[16] But the larger danger lies in exponentially increasing the violence around us. According to social scientists, seeing violence makes one more likely to act that way; people who rarely observe violence, by contrast, act violently only in the most extreme circumstances.[17]

Most troubling is the surreptitious way in which desensitization occurs. It is a gradual yet understandable reaction to an overabundance of violent imagery. Paracelsus—medieval physician, alchemist, and father of modern toxicology—once noted, "All things are poison; only the dose makes a thing not a poison." Just as the mind stores violent images and impressions, it also—as with building tolerance to poison—eventually shuts down the apparatus that alerts one to the horror of what is being seen. What other response could there be to pervasive violent imagery? It is a self-defense mechanism triggered by exposure to things the human psyche would rather not see. The problem is that by the time desensitization occurs, violence has found a home in social norms. By then, of course, it is too late.

Gauging desensitization is no easy task. Self-diagnosis is a paradox: if an individual is truly desensitized to violence, then how can he or she ever recognize heightening levels of it? Because sensitivity to violence is personal and subjective, plausible deniability is always possible; accusations from "overly sensitive" individuals fall on the deaf ears of those with high tolerances.

For these reasons, a comparative rather than objective scale must be used to measure habituation. Such scales are imperfect, but one possible means of gauging desensitization relates to how movies are evaluated and rated for content, and to a trend toward more permissive ratings, known as ratings creep. The ultraviolent movies of yesterday are standard television fare today, and moviegoers have noted that movie content has grown steadily more violent over time. Critics have long suspected that the Motion Picture Association of America (MPAA) has slackened its ratings criteria as levels of acceptability have changed, so that a PG-rated film today contains as many acts of violence as yesterday's R-rated film, and there is more risk of violent scenes being allowed in films rated G, PG, PG-13, and R than in the past. Moral guardians point to ratings creep as evidence that society is going to hell in a hurry.

Is ratings creep a real phenomenon or the manifested anxiety of over-worrisome parents? A 2004 Harvard study published in *Medscape* explores the issue, at the very least confirming its existence. Kimberly Thompson and Fumie Yokota of the Harvard School of Public Health found that movies today have more sex, violence, and profanity than similarly rated films did a decade ago. For example, *The Santa Clause* (1994) was rated PG, yet it had less sex, nudity, gore, and profanity than *The Santa Clause 2* (2002), which was rated G; *A Time to Kill* (1996), rated R, had less sex and violence than *The Lord of the Rings: The Return of the King* (2003), rated PG-13. The Harvard study also noted that more violence appeared in animated G-rated movies than in nonanimated movies. Published in the American Academy of Pediatrics journal *Pediatrics*, a 2005 study by researchers at the Southern California Injury Prevention Research Center (SCIPRC) found that some PG-rated films have more acts of violence than the average R-rated film. The MPAA provides content descriptors that specify the type of violence, language, and sexual content in every film it rates, and the SCIPRC team found that these descriptors provide a better indication of violent content than standard ratings; however, the team also concluded that the current ratings system "has failed to adhere to its definitions of the PG and PG-13 ratings, which state, 'horror and violence do not exceed moderate levels' and 'rough or persistent violence is absent,' respectively."[18]

The SCIPRC study focused on the one hundred highest-grossing films of 1994. Violent acts were divided into three levels of intensity, from "mild" shoving and slapping to nonlethal aggression to graphic deadly force. Of the top one hundred, only three films did not contain an act of violence. Perhaps the biggest surprise of the study was Disney's live-action version of *The Jungle Book*, which had the second-highest number of violent behaviors (97). (*Timecop*, starring martial-arts expert Jean-Claude van Damme, had the highest with 110.) The PG-rated retelling of the classic Rudyard Kipling tale charted more violence than *Pulp Fiction* and *Natural Born Killers*, released the same year with R ratings. Of course, the aestheticized gore of Quentin Tarantino or Oliver Stone differs considerably from Disney-fied violence, but the comparative frequency of aggression in *The Jungle Book* is still rather shocking. The study noted that violence is often used as a humorous plot device, and it is precisely this kind of violence—what media scholar George Gerbner has termed "happy violence"—that concerns students of habituation and desensitization, in addition to the over-the-top splatterfests of contemporary cinema.[19]

The SCIPRC study further noted that the MPAA's ratings criteria are somewhat nebulous, suggesting that the MPAA often decides movie ratings based on what's not there rather than what is. For example, according to MPAA criteria, a PG rating is given to films in which "explicit sex scenes and scenes of drug use are absent; nudity, if present, is seen only briefly; horror and violence do not exceed moderate levels." PG-13 ratings go to films in which "rough or persistent violence is absent; sexually oriented nudity is generally absent; some scenes of drug use may be seen; one use of the harsher sexually derived words may be heard." R-rated content is much more vague, focused on "use of language, theme, violence, sex, or . . . portrayal of drug use."[20]

Perhaps creep is inevitable under such amorphous guidelines. Only frequency and severity distinguish a PG-13 from an R rating, and because there is no higher rating in frequent use by the MPAA, the R rating is very broad. According to *Variety* writer Pamela McClintock, it encompasses "everything from a few swear words or brief flashes of nudity to repeated scenes of stomach-churning mutilation and disembowelments." Children and teens can view R-rated films with parental permission, but parents find the R rating too broad to offer meaningful guidance to kids. In 2007 the MPAA tried to rehabilitate its NC-17 rating to accommodate what are informally called "hard Rs": films with content so graphic that no one under age seventeen should be allowed to see them. A new generation of horror flicks have pushed the boundaries of the "hard R" category, but the NC-17 rating has fallen out of use—according to McClintock, the category is "virtually nonexistent for Hollywood product." Since 1990 when the rating first debuted, major studios have released only nineteen films rated NC-17, in part because of the rating's perhaps unjustified equivalence with the X rating, briefly used by the MPAA before it was hijacked by the porn industry to denote hardcore sexual content.[21]

Hollywood filmmakers traded censorship vis-à-vis the Hays

Code for a voluntary ratings system in 1968 when the MPAA began rating films. In response to charges of leniency, the MPAA revised its system in 1990 to include descriptive content; however, it has always maintained that its ratings are intended only as guidelines. While it may be true that society's moral norms are looser than they once were, ratings creep in Hollywood may or may not be evidence of such. How one views ratings creep depends on *why* ratings creep occurs. Is it a function of the decline of American civilization, as reflected in and created by Hollywood films, or is it part of a natural artistic evolution of the medium of film itself? In other words, is American society getting worse and are films reflecting the worsening, or is film itself becoming more intensely evocative as the genre evolves? One might ask whether the answer even matters with regard to the net effects of viewing violence. If audiences are increasingly sophisticated, then modern cinema still seems to groom a degree of callousness. Action films, for example, grossly manipulate audience response in scenes where viewers are invited to cheer the sadistic dispatch of villain by hero. The action film itself grew out of an American need for bigger stimulation, better violence, and faster plots, and ever-increasing levels of violence have culminated in a kind of pornoviolence: an aestheticized and pleasurable spectacle of destruction with no real dramatic purpose other than titillation.

Is there cause for concern? Perhaps. It is difficult to say how many wannabe gangsters and actual thugs live their lives as if they were living a movie, or how much the rest of us consciously or unconsciously emulate what we see on the big screen, but the fictions of Hollywood surely inform the real world in profound ways, as inner fantasies shape outer realities. In a world in which acquitted murder suspect O. J. Simpson writes a semispeculative book about the slaying of his wife entitled *If I Did It: Confessions of the Killer*, seemingly based on a make-believe video on *The Chris Rock Show* called "I Didn't Kill My Wife But Here's How I'd Do It If I Did"; in which copycat killers imitate the mayhem of a film like *Natural Born Killers* (1994), itself supposedly a satiric send-up of America's fascination with violence; or in which Eric Harris and Dylan Klebold allegedly modify a first-person-shooter game to resemble their high school, then go to the actual high school on a murderous killing spree, Baudrillard's notions of simulacra and hyperreality resonate hauntingly, with life imitating art imitating life.

As Simone Weil noted, "Imagination and fiction make up more than three-quarters of our real life."[22] For William Blake, imagination represented "the real and eternal world of which this vegetable universe is but a faint shadow."[23] If Weil and Blake were correct, then what realities do our imaginations evoke? It is true that we Americans have always enjoyed what Alex and his droogs in *A Clockwork Orange* called "a malenky bit of ultraviolence," and inevitably many of us are led deeper into the combat culture or the gun culture—into what James William Gibson has termed "warrior dreams."[24] It is quite possible that the fantasy of violence—whether the temporary escapes of action films or the head trips of armchair gladiators—may feed a level of brutality that would otherwise not exist. While it is hard to compare or to gauge where America lies in its own evolution, there are undoubtedly lessons to be learned from the Roman empire's downslide toward oblivion, as the public's interest in violent entertainment increased, as the Romans clamored for more, as their bloodlust remained unsated, and as the empire crumbled. If civilization is the opposite of barbarity then perhaps ours is, like ancient Rome, a paradox—a savage civilization.[25]

Conclusion: Rethinking Violence

> We have a bad inheritance as far as
> violence is concerned; and in recent
> years war and the mass media have
> given new vitality to the darkest strains
> in our national psyche. How can we
> master this horror in our souls before it
> rushes us on to ultimate disintegration?
> —Arthur Schlesinger Jr., *Violence* (1968)

Viosense

At this very moment it is possible to fix the problem of deadly interpersonal violence in the United States. We have not only the knowledge to curb the mayhem in our streets, schools, workplaces, and homes, but also the means to shape a society relatively free of danger and fear. We can create a peaceful, lawful nation in which the taking of human life is a shocking aberration instead of a common occurrence. This newer, better nation would require minimal sacrifice in terms of rights and liberties; in fact, it could easily exist within our current framework of laws and social mores. It would mainly entail a shift in attitude: an adjustment in how we accommodate violence in our families, in our social relations, in our entertainment, in our public spaces, in our government, and in our dealings with other sovereign nations. Such a change is not utopian fantasy. It falls well within the realm of possibility.

That's the good news. The bad news is that first we have to deal with some unpleasantries—things that most of us do not want to think about. We have to take a long, hard look at how violence manifests itself in our society. We have to face up to the ugly record of assaults, rapes, and killings happening around us.

But how? How can we deal with the limitations imposed by our own limited vantage points? The biggest impediment to positive change may be a personal one: our own inescapable sense that things must be the way they are. We wonder what we can do, already convinced that the answer is nothing. When viewing the overall pattern of societal violence, we find it difficult to make sense of the chaos. The pattern is obscure, like looking at a heavily pixilated image up close and seeing only squares. Those searching for answers in black and white may see only jumbled blocks, a checkerboard of squares in no discernible order; but, by holding the pixilated image at arm's length, a pattern emerges—a mindshift occurs. It becomes a matter of parallax, of gaining depth perception and focus. With change in positioning comes change in perspective.

The purpose of this book has been to initiate a change in perspective, to introduce alternative ways of thinking about violence—in short, as the title suggests, to rethink violence in American life. In so doing I have reached two conclusions: first, that violence negatively affects public welfare in the United States in various ways, and second, that it need not necessarily be so. In the preface I mentioned a number of assumptions about violence that we as Americans tend to embrace. My research has led me to a different set of assumptions. Human beings are *not* inherently aggressive, and men need not act violently. Watching violence can have harmful consequences. Certain forms of violent entertainment probably pollute the minds of adults as much as they do those of children. Guns tend to create more problems than they solve. War is not normative conduct between nations, no more than it is between individuals, and the world in which we live, insofar as we have control over it, is as violent as we choose to make it. Recognizing such alternatives to commonly held assumptions about violence is the core of viosense.

We Americans are collectively short on viosense and we always have been. We exhibit not only a myopic disregard of ways to address violence but also a kind of cognitive dissonance regarding its very existence. It is the pink elephant in the middle of the room. Therefore, a first step in cultivating viosense and addressing the problem is to recalibrate our comfort level with bodily harm. As is, we are far too comfortable with school shootings, violent crime, and mayhem on television. All form a kind of cultural white noise that produces cognitive dissonance and myopia in dealing with the problem. If we minimize the problem of Columbine or of Lionel Tate—if we complacently say it is all the work of psychos and criminals, that nothing is wrong—then we risk saying no to viosense and yes to violence.

In casting a blind eye on the violence that surrounds us, we have in fact perfected a kind of superviolence, actualized in gun deaths and honed in ultraviolent entertainment, that desensitizes empathy—so much so, in fact, that it becomes nearly impossible to see how destructive this violence really is. David Griffith's *A Good War Is Hard to Find: The Art of Violence in America* (2006) examines this desensitization in a thoughtful way, exploring the relationship between U.S. violence at home and abroad. Using the example of the 2004 Abu Ghraib prison scandal in Iraq, Griffith narrates a subtle, self-searching meditation on the ways that violent images sift through consciousness to affect and influence the mind in unanticipated ways. Fiction writers (and writers of creative nonfiction like Griffith) can let certain propositions hang unresolved, floating like puffs of smoke; these traces in Griffith's writing haunt the reader long after the book is put down, leaving many questions unanswered, suggesting rather than proving. The beauty of such writing lies in the white spaces in between—the inferences and hints.

For example, Griffith seems to question the Orwellian doublethink in viewing ourselves as virtuous and good while simultaneously dismissing violence committed on our behalf, in our name. When the abuse of Iraqi POWs by American guards at Abu Ghraib was revealed to the American public, it was blamed on certain "bad seeds" who committed the acts; Griffith, however, suggests that the society that enabled such an act to transpire is equally at fault. In a culture that tolerates and condones violence, we are easily drawn into participating in the very acts we claim to deplore, as Griffith does when he emulates one of the Abu Ghraib offenders at a Halloween party. As he finds himself recreating the familiar poses struck by the prison guards and captured in those incriminating photos, he becomes ashamed and vaguely horrified; for him, the cognitive dissonance is a lived reality, prompting him to reevaluate the event itself. Griffith tells us that some of his students did not see the horror in what happened at Abu Ghraib, with some saying, "What's the big deal?" and "I've seen worse." Indeed, they probably had—on television, in the movie theater, or online. Perhaps it should not be surprising that a nation enthralled by five *Saw* movies in five years (with *Saw IV* scaring up $32.1 million in a single weekend in 2007) would tacitly approve torture in intelligence gathering. Perhaps it is not such a great leap from the killing screens of Hollywood, where violence is so often portrayed without consequence or suffering, or from the pixilated video-game screens, with their astronomical body counts, to the corridors of Abu Ghraib, where the torture of detainees may have been the result of psychological processes of victim dehumanization, of tacit approval for mistreatment of prisoners, or of the belief that justice was being served.[1]

If the problems of Columbine and Abu Ghraib are somehow related, as Griffith intimates, then we must vigilantly look for ways in which the subtext of violence not only percolates into incidents of actual violence but also nurtures environments in which such violence can occur. We must consider the possible connections between seemingly disparate issues, as Griffith does, and as two important documentary films do—Michael Moore's Academy Award–winning *Bowling for Columbine* (2002) and Spencer Halpin's *Moral Kombat* (2007). We must pay as much attention to correlation as to causality. In short, we must connect the dots. Doing so represents an initial step in cultivating viosense.[2]

The Nitty-Gritty

If adjusting our perspective represents a preliminary step, then there are also a number of specific measures to address violence as a male phenomenon, as an entertainment phenomenon, as a gun phenomenon, and as a youth phenomenon. These measures are both "bottom-up," beginning with details and working up to the highest conceptual level, and "top-down," beginning with theory and working down to details. Some of them begin with the individual, others begin at the societal level. Some rely on suasion, while others rely on more programmatic institutionalization by local, state, and federal governments. Some require changes in law while others require changes in behavior. All of these measures intersect at certain points, and many of them overlap in the forms of violence that they would address.

For example, in reexamining the way in which we acculturate our children, we must also reexamine our own habits and assumptions as adults. Most of the discussion regarding not only media violence but also gun violence has revolved around ill effects on kids. But is gun violence any less harmful to adults than children? Is media violence? If one knew that media violence has harmful effects on adults, then one could safely assume that it has harmful effects on children, who are developmentally immature and morally impressionable. Still learning and still developing, they are adults in the making, susceptible to a variety of influences, good and bad. Therefore, any lessons learned about the effects of media violence on adults should apply even more strongly to children.

Until recently, we could claim ignorance. No longer can we make that claim. Evidence shows that violent images can harm us at any age. Various researchers including Craig Anderson, Brad Bushman, and Rowell Huesmann have argued that adults may be negatively influenced by exposure to media violence.[3] After testing adults exposed to a variety of violent stimuli, Leonard Berkowitz concluded, "The observation of aggression is more likely to induce hostile behavior than to drain off aggressive inclinations."[4] If *adults* are influenced by what they see, then children, who have fewer schematic reference points and fewer sources of alternative information, are perhaps even more influenced. As Joanne Cantor, professor emerita and director of the Center for Communication Research at the University of Wisconsin–Madison, notes, there are very few movies that are "safe" for children up to the age of five.[5]

What do such findings mean? At the very least they should prompt self-examination and retrospection about what we as adults find entertaining; they might further prompt a hard look at what we deem acceptable for children. How we entertain ourselves matters. One could certainly argue that Americans are so desensitized by violent entertainment as to be unable to respond to the real violence in our foreign policy, in our environment, and in our streets. If so, then the adult world poses genuine risks to young people who would live in it. As James Baldwin observed, "Children have never been very good at listening to their elders, but they have never failed to imitate them."[6]

Electronic media is one area for concern. Warning labels for films, video games, and music are appropriate and necessary. Nonviolent programming offers alternatives, while education initiatives in media literacy equip kids with the tools to view content critically. The government might provide financial incentive to television networks and the gaming industry for better programming and nonviolent video games. There is nothing problematic with video games in and of themselves; however, as part of the self-indulgent, needlessly destructive entertainments along the edges of modern American culture, *violent* video games pose certain risks, and we should recognize the possible consequences of playing violent video games just as we now recognize the ties between violent pornography and violence toward women.

One can imagine a service announcement appended to violent television shows similar to warning labels on packs of cigarettes: "Due to violent content, the following program may be hazardous to your health." Television networks might also explore what I call "TV zoning," in which violent programming is programmed out of family hours or "kid time," the hours children are most likely to watch television. In 2007, the Federal Communications Commission (FCC) concluded that reining in television violence is in the public interest, particularly during times when children are likely to be viewers (typically between 6:00 a.m. and 10:00 p.m.); since then, congressional attempts at legislation have stalled. For decades the FCC has penalized broadcasters for airing sexually suggestive, or "indecent," content, but it has never had the authority to fine TV stations and networks for violent programming. TV zoning may provide an answer. The idea derives from the growing number of cities and counties that use zoning, licensing, and other techniques to discourage strip clubs without running afoul of the First Amendment rights of club owners. The U.S. Supreme Court has ruled that cities and states can regulate adult-oriented businesses but cannot prohibit them from operating. Federal courts generally protect such businesses unless communities can prove "harmful secondary effects" such as increased crime, blight, or diminished property values; however, communities can effectively determine when and where such establishments operate. If communities can "zone out" strip clubs, then why could local television affiliates not zone out violent content?[7]

If the risks of exposure to media violence are analogous to breathing air in a smoggy city—causing cumulative damage over time—then the dangers of living in an ethos of violence may be more akin to racing the engine of an idle car in an unventilated garage. Insofar as we are what we see and know to be true, we must monitor what we take into our minds—whether images or ideas—in the same way that we have learned to monitor what we dump into the environment or ingest into our bodies. Many popular movies, for example, carry messages that violence is an appropriate male response to conflict resolution. In fact, various cultural signifiers, from westerns of the 1950s to contemporary action-adventure films, link expressions of violence with what it means to be a man. In this sense, the connections between violent entertainment and internalized understandings of gender are explicit.

As citizens of the United States, we live in a society that, as one researcher has noted, "celebrates masculinity and admires the daring and strength of its men." This celebration is evident in athletics and competition, on and off the field; in politics at home and in war overseas; in the workplace and at home; in the media and in schools—in all of the places where boys are socialized to become men. Not surprisingly, fighting and other behaviors, marginalized with the understanding that "boys will be boys," often continue when boys grow older, becoming men who continue to engage in aggressive behavior.[8]

As David Courtwright has observed, "Americans continue to think a manly man is someone with a gun and an attitude." This notion is reflected in our politics, in our child rearing, and in our entertainment, and until it changes, there is bound to be a lot of bloody gunplay in all of the above. Machismo, violent video games, hunting and shooting sports, violent movies, and more are all part of a violent male subtext in American culture and society. Some are perhaps harmless, but all must be recognized as part of an American subculture in which traditional definitions of masculinity explicitly and implicitly normalize violence for men.[9]

Violence is largely a male phenomenon. *Must* men behave this way, because of their genetic makeup? It is doubtful. Cultural norms play an enormous role in determining how people interact with their environments. If violence is not "natural," then it must be learned; if violence is learned, then it can also be unlearned. Furthermore, if violence is predominantly a male phenomenon, then any violence can be understood as a kind of sexual violence—or, more accurately, a kind of gendered violence. Presumably, then, violence can be unraveled through a new understanding of what it means to be a man. Redefining American manhood does not equate with "sissifying" boys or emasculating men. It simply means removing violence from the necessary ingredients of American manhood. It is possible to rewrite the "masculine mystique," replacing it with more open and flexible codes for male behavior. Doing so would represent an important move toward creating more meaningful relationships between boys and girls, between sons and fathers, and between men and women. Such socialization is a preliminary step in more favorably adjusting the calculus of violence and in modifying whatever tendencies men have to aggress.

Another step is moderating gun violence. Most nations strictly regulate civilian possession of firearms. The United States does not. Whether this anomaly should be a point of pride or shame is a matter of opinion, but it is clear that American citizens pay an enormously high price, in terms of private health and public safety, for such easy access to guns. If we are ever to reduce the number of school shootings, then gun violence, specifically, must hold our attention in the intervening periods between catastrophes.

On some level, dealing with guns is the easiest of all of the prescriptions for reducing violence in American society. Gun violence is the most present danger of any related to murder and mayhem. Reducing the number of guns would have the most immediate payoff in lowering homicides; in fact, there is little question that limiting or restricting public access to guns would lower the number of American citizens killed by guns each year.

Crime and lethal violence are two different animals, and while it may be possible to assert that more guns equal less violent crime, it is impossible to assert that more guns equal less lethal violence. They do not—and any efforts to address crime without addressing the separate and in many ways more troubling problem of lethal violence in the United States are incomplete and insufficient. To reduce gun violence effectively and demonstrably, one must realize there are no "right hands" and "wrong hands," no good guys and bad guys, no good guns or bad guns; rather, there is an abundance of firearms liberally distributed among a fearful, violence-prone people ready to use them against each other. In short, the more guns that circulate through a society, the greater the possibility that gun violence will occur. Considerations of right and wrong hands or good and bad guys matter little in any comprehensive violence-reduction strategy. What matters is how many guns saturate a given demographic and how many people are packing. As one team of researchers report, "Regardless of the context—crime, conflict, domestic assault, suicide—firearms increase the number of victims and the potential for children to become killers. Firearms undermine the long-term efforts to build civil society by fueling internal arms races, whether in war zones or in inner cities."[10] As Sarah Brady, whose husband James Brady was paralyzed in the 1981 assassination attempt on President Ronald Reagan, has observed, where it is easier to obtain a gun it is also easier to get shot.

It is also easier to shoot oneself. Suicides respond well to background checks and waiting periods. Experts tell us that most individuals, no matter how distraught, do not choose to shoot themselves if they have time to consider their demise. Guns enable suicide in the same way they enable other modes of lethality: that is, if a gun happens to be handy, then the chances of a successful killing go up accordingly.

Gun ownership itself is no measure of attitudes toward gun control—there are as many reasonable gun owners who would favor certain restrictions as there are nonowners who still favor the right of others to bear arms—but even if it were, there would still be little to stand in the way of major reform.

If a small minority of Americans own a majority of guns in the United States, and if that few presumes to speak for the majority in championing unabridged gun rights, then there is little that is "democratic" about continued opposition to responsible efforts to reduce gun violence. Two things are clear. First, gun control already exists in various measures; and second, if one acknowledges that a gun-violence problem exists in the United States, then those measures are only partly effective. Better regulation of guns at points of sale and transfer is an intermediate step in reducing violence, not a final measure. More laws are a poor substitute for better ones, and creative solutions may attenuate the problem of violence while simultaneously appeasing gun owners.

Gun licensing is one option. Gunner's insurance, which would require gun owners to have gun insurance in the same way that drivers need auto insurance, is another possibility; insurers might offer "safe gunner" rewards for those who do not use the gun against another person or who take an annual safety course. Government intervention in production, sales, and distribution, including importing and exporting, is another possibility, as are newer and better nonlethal weapons technologies for law enforcement and civilian use. Stricter penalties for violent crime should play a role. A "bullet tax"—that is, taxing ammunition in the same way that we tax cigarettes—might make shooting someone cost-prohibitive; such legislation was proposed in the California state legislature in 2002 by Democratic senator Don Perata. Many of these measures would require a new way of understanding gun control, as Philip J. Cook and Jens Ludwig offer in *Gun Violence: The Real Costs* (2000). Characterizing gun regulation as a "harm-reduction strategy" akin to installing air bags in motor vehicles, Cook and Ludwig recommend a number of measures such as mandating background checks on purchasers; banning small, easily concealed handguns; cracking down on illegal gun carrying; imposing stiffer sentences on those convicted of using a gun in a crime; and developing personalized "smart gun" technologies that restrict usage to particular individuals.[11]

Banning certain firearms, as was done in the United Kingdom, is yet another option, and if one were to single out a particular weapon to prohibit, the handgun—easily concealed, easily mishandled, and intended to be used against people—would be an obvious choice. A more palatable option than banning handguns might be to restrict them to certain groups, such as law enforcement officers, security guards, small business owners in high-crime areas, members of approved sporting clubs, hunters, and collectors. Banning of any sort seems unlikely given the conservative majority on the Supreme Court, which ruled in a 5-to-4 decision on June 28, 2010, that the Second Amendment's guarantee of an individual right to bear arms applies to state and local gun control laws. In a victory for gun-rights advocates, the Court ruled that even in places like Washington, D.C., and Chicago that have attempted to restrict handguns, there exists a right to keep handguns in the home for self-defense. While acknowledging that the amendment did not confer "a right to keep and carry any weapon whatsoever in any manner whatsoever and for whatever purpose," the justices looked more to the nation's violent, eighteenth-century separation from Britain and the nineteenth-century battles over slavery for proof that gun ownership is a fundamental right than they did to the present-day reality of the more than ten thousand American deaths by firearms each year.[12]

Confiscation, regulation, and control have historically been unsavory options for dealing with gun violence in the United States. Here they are dirty words, running headlong into the Second Amendment. The same can be said for censorship of media violence with regard to the first inviolable right of U.S. citizens, freedom of speech. These unsavory options are options nonetheless, and any serious discussion of violence reduction must weigh them heavily against the cost of standing idly by, doing nothing. It is a cost measured in lives lost. If regulation is unsavory, then so too was the 2002 Supreme Court decision to overturn the Child Pornography Prevention Act of 1996, which made it a crime to create, distribute, or possess "virtual" child pornography—that is, porn that uses computer images to simulate sex with minors. If regulation seems extreme or absurd, then so too are the outrageous scenarios that play out across the United States everyday, such as the actor at a Wild West theme park in northern New Jersey who shot a fellow employee in 2006 in front of an audience of parents and children during a "Sundance Kid" skit (the seventeen-year-old had inadvertently loaded his gun with .22 caliber bullets instead of blanks before shooting his colleague between the eyes); or the gunman who walked into an immigration services center in downtown Binghamton, New York, on April 4, 2009, and opened fire on a citizenship class, killing thirteen and critically wounding four others; or the 2008 death of an eight-year-old boy who accidentally shot himself in the head while taking his turn with an Uzi submachine gun at a gun show in Westfield, Massachusetts—a state that already has some of the nation's strictest gun laws.[13]

Media violence and gun violence both raise difficult questions of prescription as well as analysis. In a land based on individualism and freedom, no one wants to abridge constitutional rights or trample artistic expression. At the same time, reason must reign. Rights necessitate responsibilities, and at such point that certain constitutional freedoms inhibit public safety and general welfare, one must consider how to redefine certain problems so that they may be regulated.

Kevin Saunders, professor of law at the University of Oklahoma, has offered one possible solution. In *Violence as Obscenity: Limiting the Media's First Amendment Protection* (1996), he makes a compelling argument that certain depictions and descriptions of violence may reach such a level as to be considered—from a legal standpoint—obscene in the same way that certain depictions and descriptions of sex are. That which is deemed obscene is beyond the protection of the First Amendment; therefore, such materials would be unprotected and could be regulated, controlled, or even governmentally banned. In *Roth v. United States* (1957), the Supreme Court constructed a legal history to support First Amendment exceptions for sexually obscene materials; Saunders argues that the same sort of legal history can be constructed for a First Amendment exception for violently obscene material. The Supreme Court has historically (and erroneously, according to the Saunders) equated obscenity and pornography, but why limit obscenity to sexual activities, which are, after all, "filthy" only in certain contexts? Can death or mutilation, exhibited in a way that voids any sense of humanity, not be equally obscene—or perhaps more so? The argument hinges on the notion of "variable obscenity," a concept for addressing concerns over the exposure of adolescents to materials intended for an adult audience. Grounded in constitutional law and theory, and suggesting as it does that modern sensibilities have replaced "obscene" sex with extreme violence, Saunders's argument provides much food for thought.[14]

The difficulty in defining obscenity is best summed up by Supreme Court justice Potter Stewart, who, in the appeal of *Jacobellis v. Ohio* (1964), famously quipped, "I know it when I see it." Censorship of materials judged obscene is no less complicated. Our society nourishes a boundless popular culture that plumbs anything and everything to its extreme. In a liberal democracy in which limits, rights, and responsibilities serve as checks and balances for one another, social toxins will always puddle and pool around the edges of what we collectively deem acceptable. Indeed, pushing boundaries toward and beyond logical extremes allows us to measure, to a certain extent, what is okay and what is not. And in a society as open and tolerant as ours, there will perhaps always exist a willingness to go a little farther, to push the frontier. Sometimes artists explore such paths, sometimes crass exploiters, and sometimes both. Sometimes it is difficult to tell the difference—and for this reason censorship usually offers a Hobson's choice in dealing with objectionable content. If the risk of censoring genuine art is a possibility in censorship, then so too is the risk of elevating genuine trash. Censorship can paradoxically create deeper fascination with that which is blocked. It can also glamorize or popularize that which has little or no redeeming social value. What better shopping list for those seeking rotten extremes than a censor's blacklist?

There are other reasons to pause before stoking the bonfire. The possibility always remains that well-meaning citizens will use existing laws to legislate morality for everyone else. As Michael Leach has noted, "Censorship is objectionable because, unlike the rain, it not only sullies what it seeks to make clean, but it never falls equally on the just and on the unjust, and is therefore unjust itself."[15] The attraction of banning particularly deplorable images is as simple and clear as the purpose—to see no evil—and while few would argue against the protection of communal standards, moral values, and social order, the method of censorship—taking away choice—is more complicated and problematic, particularly in a political culture based on personal freedoms. Censorship limits choice, and choice equals freedom; therefore, censorship limits freedom. If freedom is fundamentally American, then censorship, in circumscribing choice, is distinctly un-American.

It can also have undesired effects, as explained by Karen Sternheimer. "Finger-wagging politicians and other moralizers often alienate as many members of the public as they convert," she writes, describing the ill effects of censoring video games. "In an ironic twist, they might even feed the anti-authoritarian appeal that may draw players of all ages to the games."[16] Of course, regulation need not be absolute. If the outcome of gun regulation need not be the outright banning of guns, then perhaps the outcome of censorship need not be the outright banning of materials. But if there is a way to censor "a little," then society has yet to perfect it. Censorship seems to have a way of careening toward extremes—consider book burnings, witch hunts, and the like.

A fair alternative, or perhaps a first step toward "uncensoring censorship," might be simply switching the channel—ignoring rather than suppressing. Self-censorship is a viable option, especially in an environment that provides alternatives and supports positive choices. While counterintuitive, perhaps *more* choices are better than few with regard to censorship: educating toward virtue without excluding from public view whatever we find debased or objectionable. Perhaps the only sure weapon against bad images—like bad ideas—is better ones. The best hope may be a wider realization that certain things, once seen, can never be unseen.

It is in this spirit that the Nintendo Corporation's top designer has called for more upbeat alternatives to the slew of violent but popular video games available today. Shigeru Miyamoto, who created titles such as *Mario Brothers*, *Donkey Kong*, and *The Legend of Zelda* (which have together sold about 288 million copies), is an industry guru, "the Steven Spielberg of video games," according to *Time* magazine. Miyamoto, who has worked on every Nintendo game console released over the past thirty years—including the popular Wii system—noted in 2007 that his industry's reputation has suffered in the past decade: as designers focused on hardcore gamers and their lust for gore, realism, horror, and revenge, they failed to deliver titles that bring joy to the widest possible spectrum of players. "I always want that first reaction to be positive, to give a sense of satisfaction, glee," he told an audience at the Game Developer Conference in San Francisco. "Certain obstacles may temporarily raise feelings of suspense, competition, even frustration. But we always want that final result, that final emotion, to be a positive one."[17]

The Silver Bullet

All of these particular prescriptions carry us back to the necessity of recalibrating our comfort levels, which is, in fact, a broad-spectrum solution, one that might govern particular policy decisions and more specific attempts to address violence *before* it occurs. While there is no "silver bullet," no magic cure for the problem of violence, limiting exposure is a key ingredient in changing popular opinion about the inevitability of violence and its relative harmlessness. Only in rare circumstances should we expose ourselves to graphic violence, real or imagined; violence, whether seen in two dimensions or witnessed in real life, can have lasting consequences. As individuals, as communities, and as nations, we should not initiate it without first weighing those consequences. It should be a last resort of desperation—not a surrogate for diplomacy or a first recourse of entertainment. In sum, we must limit our intake of and exposure to violence even as we are aware of our role as agents of it. As Leo Tolstoy once said, "If public opinion would but frown upon violence, it would lose all its power."[18]

But limiting exposure to violence is more than simply a matter of saying no. It also means establishing a society in which people are not always on guard. It means creating safety, strengthening social bonds, enhancing community, generating a more human poli-sphere. To acknowledge violence is to recognize how it stems from other wants—not having a steady job, not having familial support, not having safe public spaces. Therefore, on an even larger level, reducing violence entails combating poverty and ignorance.[19] This humanistic approach, changing hearts and minds, would presumably alleviate all sorts of violence through community values and education: the idea is that people are less likely to harm people they know personally. Finally, any strategy for decreasing violence must begin with strategies for increasing the value of human life, which would mean the abolishment of capital punishment.[20]

Of course, reforming the larger community necessitates protecting the home too, because we know that individuals *do* sometimes harm people they know. Statistics indicate that gun households are six times more likely to harm a family member than an intruder; domestic violence and family violence statistics show that the home is not necessarily a safe space from violence. The violence "out there" often manifests itself "in here," and in fact, the family structure sometimes enables the violence of men, hiding it behind closed doors rather than taming it. Families and "family values" are neither a corrective nor a cure-all, and domestic violence necessitates special interventions to ensure the protection of women and children from men who would harm them.

All of these prescriptions are key pieces in solving the violence puzzle. Too often we focus on a particular aspect of a problem without seeing how it relates to other issues. As soon as a specific form of violence like drive-bys or carjackings captures headlines, public attention concentrates on particulars and we lose sight of the larger problem. Until we refocus on the larger problem, it is likely there will be more murders, more elective and unnecessary wars, more schoolyard beatdowns, and more Columbines and Virginia Techs. We must widen the lens, keeping our focus deliberately blurred and imprecise.

Violence is arguably the single most pressing public health issue in the United States. Unfortunately, little is being done about it; that is, we have failed to create effective violence-prevention measures or implement policies that meaningfully reduce violence in our communities. This failure stems in part from a refusal to consider violence outside of a crime paradigm. Primary prevention—addressing violence before it happens, not after the fact—entails stopping potential aggressors from causing harm in the first place; for this reason, we must consider lethal violence apart from any crime paradigm whose best prescription is building more prisons to house criminals who have already aggressed. As correlates of violent behavior are altered (sexism, violent entertainment, alcohol abuse, weapons use, etc.), the likelihood of participating in violence diminishes; however, locking up criminals, while an effective strategy for combating repeat offenses, does little to address violence already committed.

Just as prisons are intended to keep bad guys in, gated communities are intended to keep them out; however, gated communities are a similarly spurious solution. They are a predictable and rather selfish response to the perceived problem of danger "out there." As George Gerbner has suggested, one cannot be a loving parent, providing everything that a child needs, while avoiding the duties of citizenship—the two are inherently linked—and good citizenship requires that one actively participate in building a livable society. To create a nurturing home environment one must create a vibrant, lively community defined by safe public spaces. Private enclaves, segregated from the real world, are no more of an answer than private schools, dedicated to educating a few children rather than all of our children.[21]

The United States is not the most violent nation in the world—not by a long stretch. There are less developed countries, ravaged by war and lawlessness, with higher rates of violence. The United States does, however, have the highest rates of interpersonal violence among comparable industrialized nations. Considering the richness of the United States and the historical ingenuity displayed by its people in overcoming adversity, it is shameful and embarrassing that interpersonal violence plagues this society to the degree it does. No other nation on earth holds the potential to ensure the well-being and health of all of its citizens like the United States does—and it is this potential that provides some cause for hope. If the United States does have a "bad inheritance" with regard to violence, as Arthur Schlesinger Jr. observed, then it also has a good inheritance with regard to our potential to address the problem. Schlesinger suspected as much when he wrote, "We must exert every effort to protect and strengthen the membranes of civility against the impulses of destruction."[22]

As he noted, we should never indulge in utopian fantasies of abolishing destruction or living in a violence-free society; to do so would be not only unrealistic but also undesirable. "Violence, for better or worse, *does* settle some questions, and for the better," he wrote. "Violence secured American independence, freed the slaves, and stopped Hitler."[23] Similarly, John Shelton Reed, in "Below the Smith and Wesson Line," a chapter from his book *One South: An Ethnic Approach to Regional Culture* (1982), has noted that, despite natural aversions to violence, some things are worth fighting for:

> There can be an exaggerated distaste for violence, it seems to me, which is as unwholesome in its own way as bloodlust. The pacifist merits our respect, but the coward does not. One says fighting is immoral (a defensible position, though we may disagree); the other says fighting is scary, or nasty, and nothing is worth fighting for, anyway. Whatever Southerners' faults in the matter (and they've usually been obvious), our people, black and white, have witnessed with some consistency and often at great cost to the belief that there are enemies who cannot or should not be appeased, conflicts that cannot or should not be negotiated, affronts that should not be ignored—in short, that there *are* things worth fighting for. We may disagree about what those things are, but I think we can use the reminder that they exist.[24]

It is also true that there will always be stories containing violence that will be worth telling. The point is that empty violence—whether cheap Hollywood filler or the random violence lurking in the public sphere—serves nothing, only working to diminish quality of life.

As Michael Nagler has pointed out, negativity generalizes in a person's mind, and it is important for anyone who would imbibe violence as entertainment to recognize this fact. His mantra is simple: "Violence in, violence out." If we recognized the emotional and spiritual costs of seeing violence and realized what violence was doing to us on the inside, becoming aware of how it affected our outlook on life, then we might regulate our own viewing habits. We might change our gun-toting habits. We might demand different policies from our elected officials. We might recognize our own complicity in that which we deplore.[25]

We Americans are decent folk, by and large, rightly resentful of any suggestion of wrongdoing or implication in crimes we find detestable. Yet it is not enough to find scapegoats in gun owners or video gamers or anyone else. Something is amiss, and all of us, to varying degrees, play a part in bearing witness to it. What has become normal to us is anything but to many outside our frame of reference. In fact, to many if not most peoples around the world we are a frightening force—frightening in our belligerence, frightening in our glamorization of guns, frightening in our cowboy foreign policy. If we remember the international reaction to the Virginia Tech massacre or the global outcry as we sent troops into Iraq, we remember that many peoples around the world now know us not for our ideals and values but for our inability to create peace in our prosperity. Like every act of aggression on foreign soil, every act of violence in our homeland sows doubt in American capacity for leadership. The terrible things we do to our own people and the terrible things we do to others carry much the same message.

To reduce violence requires creativity and reason, but most of all it requires cooperation. American political discourse has become so bifurcated—so divided between Democrat and Republican, liberal and conservative, red state and blue state— that real progress often seems impossible; however, there are a number of recent books that discuss the commonsensical wisdom of the middle, and one even suggests that we Americans are not nearly as divided as we think we are.[26] Perhaps this crisis can be one that Americans work together to ameliorate. Moral panic is not the answer—viosense is. As Ted Gurr writes, "In the long run I place my bet not on the intractable nature of social reality, but on the ability of Americans, in times of crisis, to take control of their lives and change what they do not like about their society."[27]

If our capacity for violence is somehow endemic, then surely we can resist it instead of giving in or—worse yet—celebrating it. If we change the way we look at things, the things we look at change. Whether or not we have the will to reduce violence in American life, we certainly have the knowledge. Whether or not we accept the consequences of violence, we certainly understand them. Whether or not we choose to live in a better world, we certainly have the desire to do so. To imagine an alternative to the violent society in which we live is as simple as it is free;

however, as Bruno Bettelheim observed, simply "agreeing that violence is bad resolves nothing."[28] Changing the ways we socialize our children, altering what we find entertaining, modifying our relationships with firearms, and strengthening communal bonds will demonstrably reduce violence in our society. Making such changes may seem daunting, but all are within the realm of possibility, and the payoff will be much greater than whatever difficulties we may anticipate. A safer, better society awaits.

Notes

Preface

1. Kim Sloan, "The danger was unfathomable . . . ," *Dalton Daily Citizen* (October 21, 2008), *www.daltondailycitizen.com / homepage / local_story_295232112.html*. For more information, see Marcus K. Gardner and Christian Boone, "Dalton Blast Work of Suicide Bomber, Authorities Say," *Atlanta Journal-Constitution* (October 17, 2008), *www.ajc.com / metro / content / metro / stories / 2008 / 10 / 17 / georgia_dalton_explosion.html*.
2. For more on the Amish school shooting, see Raymond McCaffrey, Paul Duggan, and Debbi Wilgoren, "Five Killed at Pa. Amish School," *Washington Post* (October 3, 2006).
3. See Jean Baudrillard, *Simulacra and Simulation*, trans. Sheila Faria Glaser (Ann Arbor: University of Michigan Press, 1994); for more on St. Augustine, see Sissela Bok, *Mayhem: Violence as Public Entertainment* (Reading, MA: Perseus Books, 1998), 10, 30–31.
4. Joan Burbick, *Gun Show Nation: Gun Culture and American Democracy* (New York: New Press, 2006), 12.

Introduction

1. Christine Hauser and Anahad O'Connor, "Virginia Tech Shooting Kills at Least 33," *New York Times* (April 16, 2007).
2. David Zucchino and Richard Fausset, "Feds Seek to Understand Why Shooter Used Two Guns," *Los Angeles Times* (April 17, 2007).
3. Ben Hoyle, "Vengeance Films Offer Clues to a Twisted Mindset," (London) *Times* (April 20, 2007).
4. "Campus Shootings Draw World Scrutiny," *USA Today* (April 17, 2007), *www.usatoday.com / news / nation / 2007-04-17-virginia-tech -world_N.htm*.
5. Gerard Baker, "Only the Names Change. And the Numbers," (London) *Times* (April 17, 2007); David Gardner, "A Terrible Toll in

the Country Where the Gun Is Still Sacrosanct," *Daily Mail* (April 17, 2007); "How Many More?" *Daily Mail* (April 17, 2007).

6. Charles Laurence, "The Gun Mania That Puts My Boy in Danger Every Time He Goes to School," *Daily Mail* (April 17, 2007).

7. "Weapons over the Counter," *Daily Mail* (April 17, 2007); Catherine Ellsworth, "Gun Laws: 'Most People Own a Weapon, Families Will Keep Around 27, Granny Had 13," *Daily Telegraph* (April 18, 2007).

8. Simon Jenkins, "Comment and Debate," *Guardian* (April 18, 2007); Guy Dinmore, "History Suggests Rampage Will Not Lead to Tighter Controls," *Financial Times Limited* (April 17, 2007).

9. "The American Nightmare That Goes On and On," *Yorkshire Post* (April 18, 2007); "Bloodbath Must Be a Watershed," *Yorkshire Post* (April 18, 2007).

10. "US Must Act Now on Guns," *Scottish Daily Record and Sunday Mail Ltd.* (April 17, 2007); "A Lethal Love of Guns; US Politicians Must Stand Up to Lobbyists," *Herald* (April 18, 2007); "No Escape from Horrors of America's Gun Culture," *Aberdeen Press and Journal* (April 18, 2007); "Badly Wounded, but America's Love Affair with Weapons Continues," *Irish Independent* (April 17, 2007); "Tragic Cost of US Gun Law," *Belfast Telegraph* (April 17, 2007).

11. Phillip Johnston, "On the Tough Gun Curbs in Britain," *Daily Telegraph* (April 17, 2007); Paisley Dodds, Associated Press, "Virginia Campus Shooting Shocks World and Sparks Widespread Condemnation of Gun Laws in US" (April 17, 2007).

12. "Fright to Bear Arms," *Hindustan Times* (April 17, 2007); "Your Views: The US Campus Shooting," *New Zealand Herald* (April 17, 2007); "Global Media on the Virginia Tech Shootings," *New Zealand Herald* (April 17, 2007); Hirokai Sato, "Why Can't Americans Give Up Their Guns?" *Japan Times* (August 20, 2007), available at *search. japantimes.co.jp / cgi-bin / eo20070820hs.html.*

13. Commonwealth of Virginia, Office of the Governor, *Declaration of a State of Emergency for the Commonwealth of Virginia due to Shootings at Virginia Tech*, Executive Order 49 (April 16, 2007), *www.governor.virginia.gov / Initiatives / ExecutiveOrders / 2007 / EO_49.cfm*; "Shooter's Writing Dripped with Anger," CNN News (April 18, 2007), *www.cnn.com / 2007 / US / 04 / 17 / vtech.shooting / index.html?eref=rss_education*; Maria Newman and Christine Hauser, "Panel on Virginia Tech Issues Report," *New York Times* (August 22, 2007).

14. Office of the Press Secretary, White House Press Release (April 16, 2007), *www.whitehouse.gov / news / releases / 2007 / 04 / print / 20070416-2.html*; *Report to the President on the Issues Raised by the Virginia Tech Tragedy* (June 13, 2007), *www.hhs.gov / vtreport .html#key.*

15. "Students Call For Guns in Class," News24 (August 13, 2007),

*www.news24.com/News24/World/News/0,,2-10-1462_2164057,00
.html*; Alan Boyle, "Tragedy Puts Spotlight on Tech and Training,"
MSNBC (April 18, 2007), *www.msnbc.msn.com/id/18159262/*.

16. World Health Organization, "World Report on Violence and Health,"
2002, *www.who.int/violence_injury_prevention*; U.S. Justice
Department's Bureau of Justice Statistics, "Facts at a Glance,"
www.ojp.usdoj.gov/bjs/glance/d_hmrt.htm; CDC, National Center
for Health Statistics, *Healthy People 2010, www.cdc.gov/nchs
/ppt/hpdata2010/focusareas/fa15_2_data_summary_table.xls*, all
retrieved September 4, 2007.

17. Douglas Gentile and Arturo Sesma Jr., "Developmental Approaches
to Understanding Media Effects on Individuals," in Douglas Gentile,
ed., *Media Violence and Children* (Westport, Conn.: Praeger, 2003),
21.

18. Loresha Wilson, "Shreveport Man Gets 14 Years for Shooting into
School Bus," *Shreveport Times* (April 4, 2007); "Las Vegas Teen Gets
4 Years for Shooting at School Bus," KVBC News 3 (March 1, 2007).

19. Tom Vanden Brook, "Group Puts Face on Homeless in Effort to
Reduce Assaults," *USA Today* (March 7, 2006), *www.usatoday.com
/news/nation/2006-03-07-homeless-youth_x.htm?POE=NEWISVA*;
Ashley Fantz, "Teen 'Sport Killings' of Homeless on the Rise," CNN
News (February 20, 2007), *www.cnn.com/2007/US/02/19
/homeless.attacks/index.html*. See also Nicolaus Mills, *The Triumph
of Meanness: America's War against Its Better Self* (New York:
Houghton Mifflin, 1997).

20. For more on shoejackings, see Rick Telander and Mirko Ilic,
"Senseless: In America's Cities, Kids Are Killing Kids over Sneakers
and Other Sports Apparel Favored by Drug Dealers; Who's to
Blame?" *Sports Illustrated* (May 14, 1990): 36–37; see also *Just for
Kicks: A Documentary about Sneakers, Hip-Hop, and the Corporate
Game*, DVD, dir. Thibaut de Longeville and Lisa Leone (Image
Entertainment, 2006).

21. Leslie Wolf Branscomb, "Killer's Third Try for Parole Is Rejected,"
San Diego Union-Tribune (April 18, 2001); Lance Pugmire, "San
Diego Sniper Is Denied Parole," *Los Angeles Times* (September 28,
2005).

22. Boomtown Rats, the first Irish rock band to score a #1 hit in the
United Kingdom, paved the way for bands such as U2 and the
Pogues to attain international success, though they themselves
never achieved popular success in the United States—in part
because many American radio stations hesitated to play "I Don't
Like Mondays."

23. Caitlin Lovinger, "Violence, Even Before the Internet," *New York
Times* (April 25, 1999).

24. Beth Teitell, "Road Rage: Driving Motorists to the Brink and Some

over the Edge," *Boston Herald* (January 4, 1996); John Ferri, "Road Rage: As Highways Get More Crowded and Tempers Grow Shorter, Roadway Aggression Is Spinning Out of Control," *Tampa Tribune* (March 3, 1996); "Road Rage Is Catching," *Pittsburgh Post-Gazette* (April 29, 1997); Jason Vest et al., "Road Rage," *U.S. News and World Report* (June 2, 1997); Carey Goldberg, "Out of Control Anger: As Many as 5 Percent of People Suffer from a Disorder That Can Ruin Their Lives," *Boston Globe* (August 8, 2005); Janet Cromley, "Now, Another Name for Rage," *Los Angeles Times* (June 12, 2006).

25. H. Rap Brown, quoted in Ben A. Franklin, "SNCC Head Advises Negros in Washington to Get Guns," *New York Times* (July 28, 1967).

26. On accepting violence, see J. Krishnamurti, *Beyond Violence* (New York: Harper and Row, 1973), 17.

Chapter 1

1. U.S. Department of Justice, Office of Justice Programs, Bureau of Justice Statistics, "Victim Characteristics," *www.ojp.usdoj.gov/bjs/cvict_v.htm#gender*, retrieved September 4, 2007.

2. David T. Courtwright, *Violent Land: Single Men and Social Disorder from the Frontier to the Inner City* (Cambridge, MA: Harvard University Press, 1996), 16–21.

3. Ibid., 3.

4. Ibid., 56. For similar arguments, see Roger D. McGrath, *Gunfighters, Highwaymen, and Vigilantes: Violence on the Frontier* (Berkeley: University of California Press, 1984), and John Boessenecker, *Badge and Buckshot: Lawlessness in Old California* (Norman: University of Oklahoma Press, 1988).

5. Courtwright, *Violent Land*, 21.

6. Lee H. Bowker, ed., *Masculinities and Violence* (Thousand Oaks, CA: Sage, 1998), xiv.

7. Jeffrey H. Goldstein, *Aggression and Crimes of Violence*, 2nd ed. (Oxford: Oxford University Press, 1986), 113.

8. Bowker, *Masculinities and Violence*, xv.

9. For example, see John W. Renfrew, *Aggression and Its Causes: A Biopsychosocial Approach* (Oxford: Oxford University Press, 1997). Renfrew not only surveys the psychological literature concerning aggression but also explains (and defends) his own experiments involving animal testing.

10. For more on rechanneling, see Konrad Lorenz, *On Aggression* (New York: Harcourt Brace, 1966).

11. Goldstein, *Aggression and Crimes*, 6.

12. See M. F. Ashley Montagu, ed., *Man and Aggression* (New York: Oxford University Press, 1968).

13. W. Goode, quoted in Goldstein, *Aggression and Crimes*, 14.

14. E. Anthony Rotundo, *American Manhood: Transformations in Masculinity from the Revolution to the Modern Era* (New York: Basic Books, 1993), 291.

15. Stephen J. Ducat, *The Wimp Factor: Gender Gaps, Holy Wars, and the Politics of Masculinity* (Boston: Beacon Press, 2004), 5.

16. Ibid., 5.

17. Ibid., 6.

18. Ibid., vii.

19. Ibid., 8.

20. Ibid., 21.

21. Ibid., 23.

22. Betty Friedan, *The Feminine Mystique* (1963; repr., New York: Dell, 1983), 15.

23. Bruce Feirstein, *Real Men Don't Eat Quiche: A Guidebook to All That Is Truly Masculine* (New York: Pocket Books, 1982), 15, 17.

24. Susan Jeffords, *Hard Bodies: Hollywood Masculinity in the Reagan Era* (New Brunswick, NJ: Rutgers University Press, 1994), 5.

25. Ibid., 11.

26. Susan Faludi, *Stiffed: The Betrayal of the American Man* (New York: William Morrow, 1999), 9; see also Michael Kimmel, *Manhood in America: A Cultural History* (New York: Oxford University Press, 2005).

27. Faludi, *Stiffed*, 10.

28. Ibid., 13.

29. Ibid., 37.

30. Ibid., 39.

31. Ducat, *Wimp Factor*, 49; Faludi, *Stiffed*, 102–3.

32. Faludi, *Stiffed*, 31.

33. Terrence Rafferty, review of *Falling Down*, *New Yorker* (1993), *www.newyorker.com / arts / reviews / film / falling_down_schumacher*.

34. Roger Ebert, review of *Falling Down*, *Chicago Sun Times* (February 26, 1993), *rogerebert.suntimes.com / apps / pbcs.dll / article?AID= / 19930226 / REVIEWS / 302260301 / 1023*.

35. Kelly Thornton, "He Fell Victim to His Demons: Rogue Tanker's Bizarre Act Blamed on Drugs, Alcohol," *San Diego Union-Tribune* (May 19, 1995).

36. Lorraine Adams and Dale Russakoff, "Dissecting Columbine's Cult of the Athlete," *Washington Post* (June 12, 1999); Nancy Gibbs and Timothy Roche, "The Columbine Tapes," *Time* (December 20, 1999), *www.time.com / time / magazine / article / 0,9171,992873-1,00.html*. For more on male youth violence, see James Garbarino, *Lost Boys: Why Our Sons Turn Violent and How We Can Save Them* (New York: Free Press, 1999); Nancy C. Guerra and Emilie Phillips Smith, eds., *Preventing Youth Violence in a Multicultural Society* (Washington,

DC: American Psychological Association, 2006); and Gary T. Barker, *Dying to Be Men: Youth, Masculinity, and Social Exclusion* (London: Routledge, 2005).

37. Tom Chiarella, "The Problem with Boys," *Esquire* (July 2006): 94–99.

38. Charles Derber, *The Wilding of America: How Greed and Violence Are Eroding Our Nation's Character* (New York: St. Martin's Press, 1996), 2.

39. "The Central Park Jogger Steps Forward," MSNBC (December 8, 2003), *www.msnbc.msn.com/id/3080050/print/1 /displaymode/1098.*

40. Ducat, *Wimp Factor*, 51.

41. Emilie Buchwald, Pamela R. Fletcher, and Martha Roth, eds., *Transforming a Rape Culture*, rev. ed. (Minneapolis: Milkweed Editions, 2005).

42. Deborah Prothrow-Stith and Howard R. Spivak, *Sugar and Spice and No Longer Nice* (San Francisco: Jossey-Bass, 2005), 44, 46; see also Rachel Simmons, *Odd Girl Out: The Hidden Culture of Aggression in Girls* (New York: Harcourt, 2002). For a different perspective, see Meda Chesney-Lind and Katherine Irwin, *Beyond Bad Girls: Gender, Violence, and Hype* (New York: Routledge, 2008).

Chapter 2

1. Douglas Gentile, ed., *Media Violence and Children: A Complete Guide for Parents and Children* (Westport, CT: Praeger, 2003), ix, 130.

2. Joint Statement on the Impact of Entertainment Violence on Children, Congressional Public Health Summit (July 26, 2000), *www.aap.org/advocacy/releases/jstmtevc.htm.*

3. Newton N. Minow and Craig L. LaMay, *Abandoned in the Wasteland: Children, Television, and the First Amendment* (New York: Hill and Wang, 1995), 28.

4. Steven J. Kirsh, *Children, Adolescents, and Media Violence: A Critical Look at the Research* (Thousand Oaks, CA: Sage, 2006), 168–69.

5. Michael Cieply, "Government to Take a Hard Look at Horror," *New York Times* (March 24, 2007).

6. Ben Berkowitz, Reuters, "Violent Video Games Spark Rising Debate on Bans" (February 17, 2005); Beth Winegarner, "State Politicians Proposing More Game Regulation," *GameSpot* (March 4, 2005) *www.gamespot.com/news/2005/03/04/news_6119713.html*; Redmond Carolipio, "Industry Put on Defensive," *San Bernardino*

County Sun (March 23, 2005); Associated Press, "Blagojevich Signs Bill to Restrict Sale of Mature Video Games" (July 25, 2005).

7. Federal Communications Commission Report (FCC 07-50), *In the Matter of Violent Television Programming and Its Impact on Children*, MB Docket No. 04-261 (April 25, 2007): 2; Paul Farhi and Frank Ahrens, "FCC Seeks to Rein in Violent TV Shows," *Washington Post* (April 24, 2007); Associated Press, "Blagojevich Signs Bill."

8. Jonathan Freedman, *Media Violence and Its Effects on Aggression: Assessing the Scientific Evidence* (Toronto: University of Toronto Press, 2002), 87, 43. Because his study is not comprehensive— that is, because he does not consider all studies on the subject— Freedman emphasizes that his study is not a meta-analysis; however, insofar as it is a study of studies, one may consider it as such.

9. Ibid., x.

10. Ibid., x–xi.

11. "Immortal Kombat: War Toys and Violent Video Games," in Jeffrey Goldstein, ed., *Why We Watch: The Attractions of Violent Entertainment* (New York: Oxford University Press, 1998), 67.

12. Gentile, *Media Violence and Children*, 22.

13. Eleanor Maccoby, "Effects of the Mass Media," in Otto N. Larsen, ed., *Violence and the Mass Media* (New York: Harper and Row, 1968), 120–21. Emphasis in the original.

14. Gentile, *Media Violence and Children*, 20.

15. For example, see Frederic Wertham, *A Sign for Cain: An Exploration of Human Violence* (London: Hale, 1968), 285–87; Robert Brent Toplin, *Unchallenged Violence: An American Ordeal* (Westport, CT: Greenwood Press, 1977), 196–98, 205–8; Madeline Levine, *Viewing Violence: How Media Violence Affects Your Child's and Adolescent's Development* (New York: Doubleday, 1996), 5–6, 19.

16. Loren Coleman, *The Copycat Effect: How the Media and Popular Culture Trigger the Mayhem in Tomorrow's Headlines* (New York: Paraview, 2004), 1, 251. Emphasis in the original.

17. Ibid., 202, 221, 224, 227.

18. Ibid., 163, 176, 202, 222.

19. Ibid., 256, 260.

20. Gerard Jones, *Killing Monsters: Why Children Need Fantasy, Super Heroes, and Make-Believe Violence* (New York: Basic Books, 2002), 9, 11.

21. Ibid., 41.

22. Ibid., 49–50.

23. Maria Tatar, "'Violent Delights' in Children's Literature," and Dolf Zillmann, "The Psychology of the Appeal of Portrayals of Violence," both in Goldstein, *Why We Watch*, 72, 180.

24. Jones, *Killing Monsters*, 100, 108.

25. Liam Lacey, "Dungeons and Dragons: An Underground Game Is Ready to Surface," *Globe and Mail* (November 29, 1978).

26. Diane Weathers with Donna Foote, "Beware the Harpies!" *Newsweek* (September 24, 1979): 109.

27. Mary Austin, "The Assignment: Find Out about Dungeons and Dragons," *Christian Science Monitor* (February 9, 1981): 15.

28. Anne Oman, "It's Not Just a Game, It's an Adventure," *Washington Post* (February 20, 1981).

29. Tom Zito, "In This Fantasy Land of Power and Treasure, You Don't Play Around," *Washington Post* (September 7, 1983).

30. Ibid.

31. Ibid.

32. Austin, "The Assignment."

33. Leah Y. Latimer, "Dungeons and Dragons Banned by Arlington School Board," *Washington Post* (August 19, 1983).

34. Eve Zibart, "Judge Rejects Suit Tying Suicide to Fantasy Game," *Washington Post* (October 27, 1983). After the $1 million against the high school was dismissed, the Pullings filed a $10 million lawsuit against TSR Hobbies which was also dismissed; see "Parents Sue Game's Maker," *Washington Post* (June 16, 1984).

35. William Dear, *The Dungeon Master: The Disappearance of James Dallas Egbert III* (New York: Ballantine Books, 1984), 213, 314, 212; see also Gene Lyons, "Pursuing the Dragon: *The Dungeon Master* by William Dear," *Newsweek* (November 12, 1984): 106; and Carla Hall, "Into the Dragon's Lair: Detective William Dear's Story of a Student Suicide," *Washington Post* (November 28, 1984).

36. "Young Brothers Found Dead," *Washington Post* (November 4, 1984).

37. James Brooke, "A Suicide Spurs Town to Debate the Nature of a Game," *New York Times* (August 22, 1985).

38. Jerry Adler with Shawn Doherty, "Kids: The Deadliest Game?" *Newsweek* (September 9, 1985): 93. Both BADD and the NCTV were apparently one-person operations. When Radecki resigned as research director of the NCTV in 1991, the organization folded; when Pulling died in 1997, BADD similarly ceased operations.

39. "16-Year-Old Is Convicted in Fantasy-Game Slaying of Boy, 11," *New York Times* (November 23, 1986); "In the News," *Arkansas Democrat-Gazette* (June 30, 1988).

40. Dear, *Dungeon Master*, 166.

41. Nancy Gibbs and Timothy Roche, "The Columbine Tapes," *Time* (December 20, 1999), *www.time.com / time / magazine / article /0,9171,992873-1,00.html*; Lt. Col. Dave Grossman and Gloria DeGaetano, *Stop Teaching Our Kids to Kill: A Call to Action against TV, Movie and Video Game Violence* (New York: Crown, 1999), 4.

42. Oman, "It's Not Just a Game."

43. James Paul Gee, *Why Video Games Are Good for the Soul* (Melbourne: Common Ground Publishing, 2005), 1.

44. Howard Witt, "Skip the Textbook, Play the Video Game," *Chicago Tribune* (February 11, 2007); Crystal Phend, "Video Games Hone Laparoscopic Surgery Skills," *Medpage Today* (February 19, 2007).

45. American Psychological Association Press Release (April 23, 2000), APA Online, *www.apa.org/releases/videogames.html*. For an excellent overview of violent video games, see the documentary *Moral Kombat*, dir./prod. Spencer Halplin (2007).

46. Steven J. Kirsh, *Children, Adolescents, and Media Violence*, 228.

47. Arthur Schlesinger Jr., *Violence: America in the Sixties* (New York: Signet, 1968), 57.

48. Goldstein, *Why We Watch*, 19.

49. Ibid., 19.

50. Craig Anderson, Douglas Gentile, and Katherine Buckley, *Violent Video Game Effects on Children and Adolescents: Theory, Research, and Public Policy* (Oxford: Oxford University Press, 2007), 147.

51. Victor C. Strasburger and Barbara J. Wilson, "Television Violence," in Gentile, *Media Violence and Children*, 78. Emphasis in the original.

52. Kirsh, *Children, Adolescents, and Media Violence*, 107, 109.

53. Cieply, "Government to Take a Hard Look at Horror"; David Halbfinger, "Unease in the Air and Revenge on the Screen," *New York Times* (August 26, 2007).

54. See Stephen Prince, *Savage Cinema: Sam Peckinpah and the Rise of Ultraviolent Movies* (Austin: University of Texas Press, 1998); see also Stephen Prince, *Classical Film Violence: Designing and Regulating Brutality in Hollywood Cinema, 1930–1968* (New Brunswick, NJ: Rutgers University Press, 2003), and Stephen Prince, ed., *Screening Violence* (New Brunswick, NJ: Rutgers University Press, 2000).

55. Philip French, "Violence in the Cinema," in Larsen, *Violence in the Mass Media*, 61.

56. Associated Press, "*Saving Private Ryan* Not Indecent, FCC Rules" (March 1, 2005).

57. James Agee, quoted in Michael Leach, *I Know It When I See It: Pornography, Violence, and Public Sensitivity* (Philadelphia: Westminster Press, 1975), 81.

58. Leach, *I Know It*, 85.

59. Kirsh, *Children, Adolescents, and Media Violence*, 244–45.

60. For more, see Máire Messenger Davies, *Fake, Fact, and Fantasy: Children's Interpretations of Television Reality* (Mahwah, NJ: Lawrence Erlbaum, 1997).

Chapter 3

1. Jervis Anderson, *Guns in American Life* (New York: Random House, 1984), 21.
2. Philip J. Cook and Jens Ludwig, *Guns in America: Results of a Comprehensive Survey of Gun Ownership and Use* (Washington, DC: Police Foundation, 1996).
3. David Hemenway, *Private Guns, Public Health* (Ann Arbor: University of Michigan Press, 2004), 35.
4. Garret Keizer, "Loaded," *Harper's* (December 2006): 10.
5. Ibid., 11.
6. Gregg Lee Carter, *The Gun Control Movement* (New York: Twayne, 1997), 49. These numbers may be changing. In April 2009 a survey by the Pew Research Center showed that for the first time roughly as many people said it was important to protect the rights of gun owners (45 percent) than to control gun ownership (49 percent); see Katharine Q. Seelye, "Pastor Urges His Flock to Bring Guns to Church," *New York Times* (June 26, 2009).
7. Hemenway, *Private Guns*, 6.
8. Donald Newman, quoted in Robert Brent Toplin, *Unchallenged Violence: An American Ordeal* (Westport, CT: Greenwood Press, 1975), 227.
9. Steven J. Kirsh, *Children, Adolescents, and Media Violence: A Critical Look at the Research* (Thousand Oaks, CA: Sage, 2006), 153–57.
10. *Federal Toy Gun Law* (1988), U.S. Code 15, §5001; "Police Concerned about Realistic-Looking Toy Guns," *Chicago Tribune* (March 1, 2009); Ross Thurman, "Gander Mountain Pulls 'Realistic Toy Guns,'" *Shooting Times* (March 2007), findarticles.com/p/articles/mi _m3197/is_3_52/ai_n27180112/; Marc Lacey, "In Mexico, Curbing Violence Before It Is Learned," *New York Times* (January 10, 2009). See also Sebastian Rotella, "A Latin View of American-Style Violence," *Los Angeles Times* (November 25, 1999).
11. Hemenway, *Private Guns*, 6.
12. NSSF, "Online FAQs," November 13, 2007, *www.nssf.org/industry/*.
13. Hemenway, *Private Guns*, 6–7. The legal age for purchase of a long gun is eighteen, and of a handgun, twenty-one.
14. NSSF, "Online FAQs"; Hemenway, *Private Guns*, 6–7; William J. Vizzard, *Shots in the Dark: The Policy, Politics, and Symbolism of Gun Control* (New York: Roman and Littlefield, 2000), 27, 147. Hemenway reports that household handgun ownership rose from 20 to 25 percent from 1973 to 1992; however, these numbers have apparently been in decline since.
15. Ted Schwarz, *Kids and Guns: The History, the Present, the Dangers, and the Remedies* (New York: Franklin Watts, 1999), 41–42; Philip

J. Cook and Jens Ludwig, *Gun Violence: The Real Costs* (Oxford: Oxford University Press, 2000), 15, 27; Centers for Disease Control and Prevention, National Center for Health Statistics, National Vital Statistics System, "Ten Leading Causes of Injury Death by Age Group, Highlighting Violence-Related Injury Deaths, United States—2006," *www.cdc.gov / Injury / Images / LC-Charts / 10lcViolenceRelatedInjury2006-bw-a.pdf.*

16. Hemenway, *Private Guns*, 45.

17. Ibid., 30; National Center for Injury Prevention and Control, "Fatal Firearm Injuries in the United States, 1962–1994," Violence Surveillance Summary Series No. 3, September 7, 2006, *www.cdc .gov / ncipc / pub-res / firarmsu.htm.*

18. Hemenway, *Private Guns*, 36; see also Matthew Miller and David Hemenway, "Guns and Suicide in the United States," *New England Journal of Medicine* 359, no. 10 (September 4, 2008): 989–91.

19. Wendy Cukier and Victor W. Sidel, *The Global Gun Epidemic: From Saturday Night Specials to AK-47s* (Westport, CT: Praeger Security International, 2006), xii–xvi.

20. Daniel McBride, quoted in Jane Bergman and Julia Reynolds, "The Guns of Opa-Locka," *Nation* (December 2002), *www.thenation.com / doc / 20021202 / bergman.*

21. Arthur Schlesinger Jr., *Violence: America in the Sixties* (New York: Signet, 1968), 47.

22. Cook and Ludwig, *Gun Violence*, 33.

23. Franklin E. Zimring and Gordon Hawkins, *Crime Is Not the Problem: Lethal Violence in America* (New York: Oxford University Press, 1997), 52.

24. Jack Miles, quoted in Nicolaus Mills, *Arguing Immigration: The Debate over the Changing Face of America* (New York: Touchstone, 1994), 111.

25. Hemenway, *Private Guns*, 27–28.

26. Katharine Mieszkowski, "Barbie's Home Ruled a Toxic Site," *Salon* (September 6, 2007); Jad Mouawad, "550,000 More Chinese Toys Recalled for Lead," *New York Times* (September 27, 2007); "Accidental Shooting Victim Identified," *Eagle Herald* (August 30, 2007), *www.eagleherald.com / npgo0831.asp;* "16-Year-Old Killed in Accidental Shooting," KRQE News 13 (September 7, 2007), *www.krqe.com / Global / story.asp?S=7041069;* KFOR-TV, "Three Police Officers Fired over Accidental Shooting" (October 9, 2007), *www.kfor.com / Global / story.asp?S=7189691;* "Teenager Dies from Shot to Chest After He and Friend Play with Loaded Rifle," *FortBendNow* (September 17, 2007), *www.fortbendnow.com / news / 3359 / teenager-dies-from-shot-to-chest-after-playing-with -loaded-rifle;* "Father's Misplaced Gun Kills Ceres Toddler" ABC News 10, Sacramento (September 20, 2007), *www.news10*

.net / display_story.aspx?storyid=32912; "Tifton Teen Dead After Accidental Shooting," WALB News (September 23, 2007), *www.walb.com / Global / story.asp?S=7117334&nav=5kZQ*; "Teen Dies in Accidental Shooting," *Tulsa World* (September 23, 2007), *www.tulsaworld.com / news / article .aspx?articleID=070923_1_A5_spanc22342*.

27. CDC, *Morbidity and Mortality Weekly Report* 41, no. 25 (June 26, 1992): 442–45, 451, *www.cdc.gov / mmwr / preview / mmwrhtml / 00017018.htm*. For more on Eddie Eagle and the NRA's GunSafe Program, see *www.nrahq.org / safety / eddie /*.

28. Schwarz, *Kids and Guns*, 41-42.

29. Ibid., 44, 50–51.

30. Ibid., 46.

31. Ibid., 28.

32. Joseph F. Sheley and James D. Wright, *In the Line of Fire: Youth, Guns, and Violence in Urban America* (New York: Aldine de Gruyter, 1995), 135.

33. Ibid., xii.

34. Ibid., 151–52.

35. Ibid., 161.

36. Marianne W. Zawitz, U.S. Deparment of Justice, Office of Justice Programs, Bureau of Justice Statistics, "Guns Used in Crime: Firearms, Crime, and Criminal Justice," NCJ-148201 (July 1995): 1–7, *bjs.ojp.usdoj.gov / index.cfm?ty=pbdetail&iid=947*; Michael R. Rand, U.S. Deparment of Justice, Office of Justice Programs, Bureau of Justice Statistics, "Guns and Crime: Handgun Victimization, Firearm Self-Defense, and Firearm Theft," NCJ-147003 (April 1, 1994), *bjs.ojp.usdoj.gov / index. cfm?ty=pbdetail&iid=946*.

37. John Lott, *More Guns, Less Crime: Understanding Crime and Gun Control Laws* (Chicago: University of Chicago Press, 1998). One reviewer in the *New England Journal of Medicine* compared Lott's analysis to Archie Bunker's solution to the hijacking problem of the 1970s: "If everyone was allowed to carry guns, them hijackers wouldn't have no superiority. All you gotta do is arm all the passengers, then no hijacker would risk pullin' a rod." David Hemenway, "Making a Killing: The Business of Guns in America," *New England Journal of Medicine* 339 (December 31, 1998): 2029.

38. Joyce Lee Malcolm, *Guns and Violence: The English Experience* (Cambridge, MA: Harvard University Press, 2004).

39. For a discussion of research on guns in the home as a risk factor, see Bob Thompson, "Trigger Points: The Science of Violence," *Washington Post Magazine* (March 29, 1998), *www.washingtonpost .com / wp-srv / national / longterm / trigger / trigger1.htm*.

40. A federal ban on assault weapons, part of the Violent Crime

Control and Law Enforcement Act of 1994, expired in 2004 as part of the law's sunshine provision; efforts to reinstitute a federal ban continue.

41. Leonard Berkowitz, "Impulse, Aggression, and the Gun," *Psychology Today* 2 (1968): 22; anonymous interviewee, quoted in Jennifer L. Hochschild, *Facing Up to the American Dream: Race, Class, and the Soul of the Nation* (Princeton, NJ: Princeton University Press, 1995), 201; Zimring and Hawkins, *Crime Is Not the Problem*, 160–61; Scott Phillips and Michael O. Maume, "Have Gun Will Shoot?" *Homicide Studies* 11, no. 4 (2007): 272–94; Desmond P. Ellis, Paul Weinir, and Louie Miller III, "Does the Trigger Pull the Finger? An Experimental Test of Weapons as Aggression-Eliciting Stimuli," *Sociometry* 34, no. 4 (1971): 453–65; Jeffrey Goldstein, *Aggression and Crimes of Violence*, 2nd ed. (New York: Oxford University Press, 1986), 75, 91–92.

42. Charlton Heston, "The Second Amendment: America's First Freedom," address to the National Press Club, September 11, 1997, reprinted in Jan E. Dizard, Robert Merrill Muth, and Stephen P. Andrews Jr., eds., *Guns in America: A Reader* (New York: New York University Press, 1999), 199.

43. Keizer, "Loaded," 10.

44. Vizzard, *Shots in the Dark*, xvii; Gary Kleck and Don B. Kates, *Armed: New Perspectives on Gun Control* (Amherst, NY: Prometheus Books, 2001), 110.

45. Kleck and Kates, *Armed*, 129.

46. Cook and Ludwig, *Gun Violence*, viii, 65.

47. Ibid., 42.

48. Hemenway, *Private Guns*, 9, 24.

49. Ibid. For a different perspective, see Kleck and Kates, *Armed*, 32–35, 57. "No doubt health advocates genuinely desire that gun death be reduced," writes Kates. "But that desire is constantly compromised by a hatred of guns which precludes serious consideration of any option other than reducing gun ownership as a way of reducing firearms fatalities."

50. Cook and Ludwig, *Gun Violence*, 57.

Chapter 4

1. Gavin de Becker, *The Gift of Fear: Survival Signals That Protect Us from Violence* (New York: Dell, 1997), 7.

2. L. Jon Wertheim, excerpt from *Blood in the Cage*, SI.com (January 21, 2009), *sportsillustrated.cnn.com / 2009 / writers / the _bonus / 01 / 20 / blood-in-the-cage / index.html*. For more on MMA, see Wertheim, *Blood in the Cage: Mixed Martial Arts, Pat Miletich, and*

the Furious Rise of the UFC (New York: Houghton Mifflin, 2009); see also Sam Sheridan, *A Fighter's Heart: One Man's Journey through the World of Fighting* (New York: Grove Press, 2008).

3. L. Jon Wertheim, "The New Main Event," *Sports Illustrated* (May 28, 2007), *vault.sportsillustrated.cnn.com / vault / article / magazine / MAG1108589 / index.htm?eref=sisf*; see also David Sweet, "SportsBiz: How UFC Crushed Its Competition," MSNBC (November 5, 2008), *www.msnbc.msn.com / id / 27562254 /*.

4. Pat Miletich, quoted in Wertheim, "The New Main Event."

5. Wertheim, "The New Main Event."

6. For more on bare-knuckle prizefighting, see Elliot J. Gorn, *The Manly Art: Bare-Knuckle Prize Fighting in America* (Ithaca, NY: Cornell University Press, 1986). For more on boxing deaths, see "Johnson Death Sparks Angry Debate," BBC Sport (September 23, 2005), *news.bbc.uk / go / pr / fr / - / sport1 / hi / boxing / 4275652.stm*. For comparisons between boxing and MMA, see Peter Duffy, "Banned Sport Gains Fans, and Seeks More in Albany," *New York Times* (January 21, 2009).

7. For example, see Pat Muir, "Backyard Brawls Morph into E. Washington Blood Sport," KOMO-TV (March 23, 2008), *www.komonews.com / news / local / 16938816.html*.

8. April Thompson, "Teens Posting Fight Video on Web, What's Behind the Trend?" WREG-TV News Channel 3 (April 30, 2008), *www.wreg.com / global / story.asp?s=8252340*; "Violent Attacks Filmed on Phone," BBC News (February 22, 2006), *news.bbc.co.uk / go / pr / fr / - / 2 / hi / uk_news / england / london / 4739608.stm*.

9. "Web Child Fight Videos Criticized," BBC News (July 29, 2007), *news.bbc.co.uk / go / pr / fr / - / 2 / hi / uk-news / 6920817.stm*; Peter Whoriskey, "YouTube Bans Videos That Incite Violence," *Washington Post* (September 12, 2008); Caroline Heldman, "YouTube Nation," unpublished paper, *www.apsanet.org / ~lss / Newsletter / jan07 / Heldman.pdf*, retrieved November 13, 2009; Raphael Rowe, "Children's Fight Club," BBC News (July 29, 2007), *news.bbc.co.uk / go / pr / fr / - / hi / programmes / panorama / 6921555.stm*.

10. Daren Fonda, "Suburban Smackdown," *Time* (June 26, 2000); Dana Canedy, "Boy Convicted of Murder in Wrestling Death," *New York Times* (January 26, 2001).

11. Associated Press, "Kids as Young as 6 Engage in Ultimate-Fighting Craze," *Palm Beach Post* (March 29, 2008).

12. Ryan Schmidt, quoted in Greg Auman, "A Rep for Brutality," *St. Petersburg Times* (December 31, 2007), *www.sptimes.com / 2007 / 12 / 31 / news_pf / Sports / A_rep_for_brutality.shtml*.

13. Mike Simmonds, quoted in Auman, "A Rep for Brutality."

14. Michael S. Schmidt, "NFL's Vick Accepts Plea Deal in Dog-Fight Case," *New York Times* (August 20, 2007).

15. "'Bumfight' Videos Inspired Joy-Killing," CBS News (October 1, 2006), *www.cbsnews.com / stories / 2006 / 09 / 28 / 60minutes / main2049967.shtml*.

16. Dolf Zillman, "The Psychology of the Appeal of Portrayals of Violence," in Jeffrey Goldstein, ed., *Why We Watch: The Attractions of Violent Entertainment* (New York: Oxford University Press, 1998), 183.

17. Jeffrey Goldstein, *Aggression and Crimes of Violence* (Oxford: Oxford University Press, 1986), 110.

18. Kimberly M. Thompson and Fumie Yokota, "Violence, Sex, and Profanity in Films: Correlation of Movies Ratings with Content," *Medscape* 6, no. 3 (2004): 3, *www.medscape.com / viewarticle / 480900*; Lucille Jenkins et al., "An Evaluation of the Motion Picture Association of America's Treatment of Violence in PG-, PG-13-, and R-Rated Films," *Pediatrics* 115, no. 5 (May 2005): 512–17.

19. Steve Pearsall, "Hollywood's Real Dark Side: 'Ratings Creep,'" *St. Petersburg Times* (May 13, 2005), *www.sptimes.com / 2005 / 05 / 13 / news_pf / Floridian / Hollywood_s_real_dark.shtml*; Jennifer Harper, "Film Ratings for Violence Labeled as Meaningless," *Washington Times* (May 3, 2005), *www.washingtontimes.com / news / 2005 / may / 03 / 20050503-122314-4473r /*.

20. Pearsall, "Hollywood's Real Dark Side."

21. Harper, "Film Ratings for Violence"; Pamela McClintock, "MPAA Tries to Remove NC-17 Stigma," *Variety* (March 10, 2007), *www.variety.com / article / VR1117960864.html*.

22. Simone Weil, *Gravity and Grace*, new ed. (New York: Routledge Classics, 2002), 56.

23. S. Foster Damon and Morris Eaves, *A Blake Dictionary: The Ideas and Symbols of William Blake*, rev. ed. (Providence: Brown University Press, 1988), 195.

24. See James William Gibson, *Warrior Dreams: Paramilitary Culture in Post-Vietnam America* (New York: Hill and Wang, 1994).

25. Joe Contreras and Owen Matthews, "If Lethal Dictators Ban the Death Penalty, Who Cares?" *Newsweek* (April 14, 2008).

Conclusion

1. David Griffith, *A Good War Is Hard to Find: The Art of Violence in America* (Brooklyn: Soft Skull Press, 2006).

2. *Bowling for Columbine*, DVD, dir. Michael Moore (MGM, 2003). *Moral Kombat*, which won a Director's Choice Award at the Dallas Film and Video Festival, has been screened at various film festivals; it is available for download through Amazon OnDemand, Netflix, iTunes, and Hulu. See Bija Gutoff, "'Moral Kombat': Documenting

the Game Industry," *www.apple.com / ca / pro / video / halpinkatrib / index.html*; see also "Moral Kombat Movie Trailer Released—Film Explores Game Violence Controversy," GamePolitics (January 3, 2007), *gamepolitics.com / 2007 / 01 / 03 / moral-kombat-movie-trailer -released-film-explores-game-violence-controversy.*

3. In 1986, Jeffrey H. Goldstein noted, "Even while recognizing that violence on television is fictional and staged, adults too have been found to become more aggressive following exposure to media violence"; however, he has since recanted, saying that the evidence does not actually support this statement. See Goldstein, *Aggression and Crimes of Violence*, 2nd ed. (New York: Oxford University Press, 1986), 44–45.

4. Leonard Berkowitz, quoted in Michael Leach, *I Know It When I See It: Pornography, Violence, and Public Sensitivity* (Philadelphia: Westminster Press, 1975), 96.

5. Joanne Cantor, quoted in "What Makes a Kid's Movie Scary," *New York Times* (October 16, 2009).

6. James Baldwin, *Nobody Knows My Name* (New York: Dell, 1961), 59.

7. Paul Farhi and Frank Ahrens, "FCC Seeks to Rein in Violent TV Shows," *Washington Post* (April 24, 2007).

8. Luoluo Hong, "Redefining Babes, Booze and Brawls: Men against Violence—Towards a New Masculinity" (PhD diss., Louisiana State University, 1998), 8.

9. David Courtwright, *Violent Land: Single Men and Social Disorder from the Frontier to the Inner City* (Cambridge, MA: Harvard University Press, 1998), 4.

10. Wendy Cukier and Victor W. Sidel, *The Global Gun Epidemic: From Saturday Night Specials to AK-47s* (Westport, CT: Praeger Security International, 2006), xv.

11. Philip J. Cook and Jens Ludwig, *Gun Violence: The Real Costs* (New York: Oxford University Press, 2000), 30; "State Senator Calls for Tax on Bullets," KGTV–San Diego (March 29, 2002), *www.10news .com / print / 138845 / detail.html.*

12. Adam Liptak, "Justices Extend Firearm Rights in 5-to-4 Ruling," *New York Times* (June 28, 2010).

13. Linda Greenhouse, "'Virtual' Child Pornography Ban Overturned," *New York Times* (April 17, 2002); Caren Chesler, "Shooting Case Still Hangs over Wild West Park," *New York Times* (September 16, 2008); Robert D. McFadden, "13 Shot Dead during a Class on Citizenship," *New York Times* (April 4, 2009); Katie Zezima, "Police Chief among 4 Indicted in Boy's Death at Gun Show," *New York Times* (December 4, 2008).

14. Kevin W. Saunders, *Violence as Obscenity: Limiting the Media's First Amendment Protection* (Durham, NC: Duke University Press, 1996).

15. Michael Leach, *I Know It When I See It: Pornography, Violence, and Public Sensitivity* (Philadelphia: Westminster Press, 1975), 109.

16. Karen Sternheimer, "Do Video Games Kill?" *Contexts* 6, no. 1 (Winter 2007): 16.

17. Rachel Konrad, "Nintendo Guru Wants More Happy Games," *Brisbane Times* (March 8, 2007), *news.brisbanetimes.com.au /technology/nintendo-guru-wants-more-happy-games-20070309-1cp .html*.

18. Leo Tolstoy, *The Complete Works of Lyof N. Tolstoï* (New York: Thomas Y. Crowell, 1899), page unknown.

19. For more, see Barbara H. Chasin, *Inequality and Violence in the United States: Casualties of Capitalism* (Amherst, NY: Humanity Books, 2004).

20. For violence reduction strategies, see Robert L. Hampton, Pamela Jenkins, and Thomas P. Gullotta, eds., *Preventing Violence in America* (Thousand Oaks, CA: Sage, 1996); Michael N. Nagler, *Is There No Other Way? The Search for a Nonviolent Future* (Berkeley, CA: Berkeley Hills Books, 2001); Mary Wynne Ashford with Guy Dauncey, *Enough Bloodshed: 101 Solutions to Violence, Terror, and War* (Gabriola Island, BC: New Society, 2006); and John Keane, *Violence and Democracy* (Cambridge: Cambridge University Press, 2004).

21. George Gerbner, in *The Killing Screens: Media and the Culture of Violence*, DVD, dir. Sut Jhally (Media Education Foundation, 1996).

22. Schlesinger, *Violence*, 63.

23. Schlesinger, *Violence*, 39.

24. John Shelton Reed, *One South: An Ethnic Approach to Regional Culture* (Baton Rouge: Louisiana State University Press, 1982), 153.

25. Nagler, *Is There No Other Way?* 27, 34.

26. For example, see Ted Halstead, *The Radical Center: The Future of American Politics* (New York: Anchor Books, 2002); Mark Satin, *Radical Middle: The Politics We Need Now* (Boulder, CO: Westview Press, 2004); and John Avlon, *Independent Nation: How Centrism Can Change American Politics* (New York: Harmony Books, 2004).

27. Ted Gurr, ed., *Violence in America: The History of Crime* (Newbury Park, CA: Sage, 1989), 19.

28. Bruno Bettelheim, "Violence: A Neglected Mode of Behavior," *Annals of the American Academy of Political and Social Science* 364 (March 1966): 51.

Bibliographic Essay

There is no shortage of academic writing on violence in American life. Constitutional experts and historians have written about the origins of the right to bear arms, the historic prominence of firearms in American folklore and myth, and the contemporary gun culture. Biologists and psychologists have examined the propensity of humans to aggress. Experts in women's studies have offered feminist perspectives on how violent behavior is socialized, particularly in men. Criminologists have treated violent crime, while other scholars have described the potentially toxic effects of new media such as cable television, video games, and the Internet.

Few scholars, however, have tackled all of these subjects together—at least not in recent years. Not since Robert Brent Toplin's *Unchallenged Violence: An American Ordeal* (Westport, CT: Greenwood, 1975) has any writer presented a comprehensive exploration of the manifestations and sources of violence in the United States. Toplin's was the last book in an explosion of scholarly output on violence in the 1960s and 1970s. In the wake of race riots during the "long, hot summers" of the 1960s, the assassinations of key public figures such as John F. Kennedy and Martin Luther King Jr. during these same years, a preoccupation with law and order during the Johnson and Nixon administrations, and the national ordeal of the war in Vietnam, American scholars focused intently on what they identified collectively as "the problem of violence." These analyses, which tended to be broad in focus, were plentiful. Arthur Schlesinger Jr. pondered the bloody events of America's recent past in *Violence: America in the Sixties* (New York: New American Library, 1968). The first two task reports of President Johnson's National Commission on the Causes and Prevention of Violence—Hugh Davis Graham and Ted Robert Gurr's *Violence in America* (Washington, DC: U.S. Govt. Printing Office, 1969) and Jerome Skolnick's *The Politics of Protest* (Washington, DC: U.S. Govt. Printing Office, 1969)—enjoyed wide re-printing and circulation in paperback editions in 1969. The fol-lowing year, Hannah Arendt offered a classic exploration of the relationship between not only war and politics but also violence and power in *On Violence* (New York: Harcourt, Brace and World, 1970). Alphonso Pinkney wrote his excellent *The American Way of Violence* (New York: Random House) in 1972, and in 1975 Richard Maxwell Brown provided a historical explanation of the roots of American disorder in *Strain of Violence* (New York: Oxford Univer-sity Press). Toplin's *Unchallenged Violence* still represents the best general treatise on the etiology of violence. These works represent a sampling of the outpouring of scholarship on violence, broadly considered.

Interestingly, since Toplin, scholars have tended to focus more on specific issues rather than on violence as an overarching phe-nomenon in American life. Today it is more popular to investigate particular aspects of American violence—gangs or terrorism or crime, for example—than to investigate violence on the whole. There is certainly a need for specified studies, a need which may never abate; however, because violence, working in explicit and implicit ways, permeates the lives of all Americans on a daily ba-sis, there is also a need for wider, synthetic works that attempt to address it as a sweeping theme in American life. Such inquiries can provide the necessary grounding for a recalibration of com-mon attitudes about the inevitability and unavoidability of vio-lence. They can also provide a much-needed framework to conjoin the existing works in related fields.

In the past decade, the best books on violence have sought to reconfigure the parameters of public dialogue. Joan Burbick's *Gun Show Nation: Gun Culture and American Democracy* (New York: New Press, 2007), for example, avoids the tired debate be-tween pro- and anti-gun-control forces to examine the core beliefs of American gun owners. Debra Neihoff's *The Biology of Violence* (New York: Free Press, 2002) and John W. Renfrew's *Aggression and Its Causes: A Biopsychosocial Approach* (New York: Oxford University Press, 1997) represent attempts by behavioral scien-tists to move neuroscience beyond genetics and the medicaliza-tion of violence. Texts such as Kevin W. Saunders's *Violence as Obscenity: Limiting the Media's First Amendment Protection* (Dur-ham, NC: Duke University Press, 1996), Franklin E. Zimring and

Gordon Hawkins's *Crime Is Not the Problem: Lethal Violence in America* (New York: Oxford University Press, 1997), and David Hemenway's *Private Guns, Public Health* (Ann Arbor: University of Michigan Press, 2004) point the way toward reconceptualizing specific issues; these works demonstrate how to construct a legal history to support a First Amendment exception for not only sexually obscene materials but also violently obscene materials, how to define violence apart from a crime paradigm, and how to understand gun violence as a public health issue, respectively.

As impressive as these studies are, they are still pieces in a larger puzzle, and whatever comment they make about violence in general is largely incidental; that is, each still concentrates on a specific element, be it guns or neurobiology or violent movies. While eye-opening and even essential, they still tend to center on "micro" topics rather than on the "macro" subject of violence. Because a society can effectively solve specific violence-related problems without solving the larger problem of violence, there is still a need for a macro-discussion of violence. To put it another way, one can treat symptoms without curing the disease. For example, in the 1980s drive-by shootings were a particular menace, and in the 1990s carjackings; yet while law enforcement effectively met these specific threats, violence remained, manifesting itself in new and different ways. To combat the onerous effects of violence, a society must not only begin a dialogue but also effectively *create a language* to discuss broad-spectrum violence, to recognize how it pervades society, and to decide what is acceptable and what is not. The parable of the blind men accurately describing parts of an elephant without accurately identifying the animal reminds us of this need.

Perhaps there exists a need for a new etiological work, one that situates violence in an American context by utilizing the notion of *ethos*, from the Greek word for custom or character. If an ethos describes the distinguishing sentiment, moral nature, or guiding beliefs of a person, group, or institution, then the easy way in which Americans embrace the use of force surely captures this nation's ethos of violence. This new work should be, in essence, a meta-analysis of violence in the United States, presented in a readable, accessible way for a general audience.

Have writers such as Toplin not already covered this ground? Yes and no. Toplin's observations are as perspicacious today as they were in 1975, when he expertly described the American ethos of violence. His theory of avoidance, which posits that living in a violence-ridden culture fosters hiding from reality, continues to illuminate the difficulty of acknowledging the problem. His scholarship provides a kind of baseline for studying violence, and any new etiological examination must echo its concerns while updating its content and focus. Toplin wrote about the concerns of the day: street crime, racial antagonisms, assassinations, and nonpeaceful protests receive extended consideration in his work. While these concerns have not disappeared, they have certainly been overshadowed as of late by a host of new concerns: school shootings, violent video games, cyber-bullying, and gun control, for example. Like Toplin's work, any new etiological work must zero in on the normalization of violence. Of particular interest is how violence has transmogrified from aberrant behavior into everyday occurrence in the United States. How has violence become so integrated into the culture, so much a part of the way of life, that Americans often view it as a commonplace event? Accordingly, the work should focus less on why hardened criminals and terrorists do what they do and more on how otherwise law-abiding citizens are drawn into increasingly violent patterns of association—that is, less on pathology and more on the normalcy of violence. Understanding this normalcy is crucial in jogging many of us out of our comfort zones, in getting us to think critically about our own beliefs, and perhaps even in changing our minds. To address the problem we must first see it and acknowledge it. In understanding the normalcy of violence, we can appreciate just how abnormal it really is.

A number of books have already proved helpful toward this end. On men and violence, see David T. Courtwright's *Violent Land: Single Men and Social Disorder from the Frontier to the Inner City* (Cambridge, MA: Harvard University Press, 1996) and Lee H. Bowker's *Masculinities and Violence* (Thousand Oaks, CA: Sage, 1998). For more information on masculinity and the construction of gender, see E. Anthony Rotundo's *American Manhood: Transformations in Masculinity from the Revolution to the Modern Era* (New York: Basic Books, 1993), Stephen J. Ducat's *The Wimp Factor: Gender Gaps, Holy Wars, and the Politics of Masculinity* (Boston: Beacon Press, 2004), Susan Jeffords's *Hard Bodies: Hollywood Masculinity in the Reagan Era* (New Brunswick, NJ: Rutgers

University Press, 1994), Michael Kimmel's *Manhood in America: A Cultural History* (New York: Oxford University Press, 2005), Ingeborg Breines, Robert Connell, and Ingrid Eide's (eds.) *Male Roles, Masculinities, and Violence: A Culture of Peace Perspective* (Paris: Unesco, 2000), and Susan Faludi's *Stiffed: The Betrayal of the American Man* (New York: William Morrow, 1999). Various authors in Emilie Buchwald, Pamela R. Fletcher, and Martha Roth's (eds.) *Transforming a Rape Culture* (Minneapolis: Milkweed Editions, 2005) offer feminist perspectives on how male violence degrades quality of life. On the ways young women model male violence, see Deborah Prothrow-Stith and Howard R. Spivak's *Sugar and Spice and No Longer Nice* (San Francisco: Jossey-Bass, 2005) and Rachel Simmons's *Odd Girl Out: The Hidden Culture of Aggression in Girls* (New York: Harcourt, 2002); for a different perspective, see Meda Chesney-Lind and Katherine Irwin's *Beyond Bad Girls: Gender, Violence, and Hype* (New York: Routledge, 2008).

The literature on aggression is plentiful. Classic introductions to the topic include Konrad Lorenz's *On Aggression* (New York: Harcourt, 1966) and M. F. Ashley Montagu's *Man and Aggression* (New York: Oxford University Press, 1968). Debra Neihoff's *The Biology of Violence* (2002) and John W. Renfrew's *Aggression and Its Causes: A Biopsychosocial Approach* (1997) offer newer interpretations. The best refutation of biological explanations of the causes of aggression is Jeffrey H. Goldstein's *Aggression and Crimes of Violence* (Oxford: Oxford University Press, 1986).

Much has been written about the effects of media violence. On children and media violence, see Newton N. Minow and Craig L. LaMay's *Abandoned in the Wasteland: Children, Television, and the First Amendment* (New York: Hill and Wang, 1995), Madeline Levine's *Viewing Violence: How Media Violence Affects Your Child's and Adolescent's Development* (New York: Doubleday, 1996), Gerard Jones's *Killing Monsters: Why Children Need Fantasy, Super Heroes, and Make-Believe Violence* (New York: Basic Books, 2002), Craig Anderson, Douglas Gentile, and Katherine Buckley's *Violent Video Game Effects on Children and Adolescents: Theory, Research, and Public Policy* (Oxford: Oxford University Press, 2007), Diane Ravitch and Joseph P. Viteritti's *Kid Stuff: Marketing Sex and Violence to America's Children* (Baltimore: Johns Hopkins University Press, 2003), and William A. Belson's *Television Violence and the Adolescent Boy* (Farnborough, UK: Saxon House, 1978). Most helpful are Douglas Gentile's *Media Violence and Children: A Complete Guide for Parents and Children* (Westport, CT: Praeger, 2003) and Steven J. Kirsh's *Children, Adolescents, and Media Violence: A Critical Look at the Research* (Thousand Oaks, CA: Sage, 2006). Other interesting works in this field include Seymour Feshbach's and Robert D. Singer's *Television and Aggression* (San Francisco: Jossey-Bass, 1971), Jonathan Freedman's *Media Violence and Its Effects on Aggression: Assessing the Scientific Evidence* (Toronto: University of Toronto Press, 2002), Cynthia Carter and C. Kay Weaver's *Violence and the Media* (Philadelphia: Open University Press, 2003), Jeffrey Goldstein's *Why We Watch: The Attractions of Violent Entertainment* (New York: Oxford University Press, 1998), Loren Coleman's *The Copycat Effect: How the Media and Popular Culture Trigger the Mayhem in Tomorrow's Headlines* (New York: Paraview, 2004), and James Paul Gee's *Why Video Games Are Good for the Soul* (New York: P. Lang, 2005). Sut Jhally's documentary film *The Killing Screens: Media and the Culture of Violence* (1996) is also helpful, as is Spencer Halpin's *Moral Kombat* (2007).

Otto Larsen's *Violence in the Mass Media* (New York: Harper and Row, 1968), while older, still provides excellent insights. Stephen Prince has written three definitive books on screen violence in Hollywood; see *Savage Cinema: Sam Peckinpah and the Rise of Ultraviolent Movies* (Austin: University of Texas Press, 1998), *Screening Violence* (New Brunswick, NJ: Rutgers University Press, 2000), and *Classical Film Violence: Designing and Regulating Brutality in Hollywood Cinema, 1930–1968* (New Brunswick, NJ: Rutgers University Press, 2003). Michael Leach's *I Know It When I See It: Pornography, Violence, and Public Sensitivity* (Philadelphia: Westminster Press, 1975) is an elegant and eloquent book, still the best on the subject.

Some of the best books on the gun culture are older ones. Robert Sherrill's *The Saturday Night Special, and Other Guns with Which Americans Won the West, Protected Bootleg Franchises, Slew Wildlife, Robbed Countless Banks, Shot Husbands Purposely and by Mistake, and Killed Presidents—Together with the Debate over Continuing Same* (New York: Charterhouse, 1973) is a lively, entertaining, yet devastating look at the gun culture in the United States; Jervis Anderson's *Guns in American Life* (New York: Random House, 1984) is also particularly well written and insightful. Other notable books in this field include Gregg Lee Carter's

The Gun Control Movement (New York: Twayne, 1997), William J. Vizzard's *Shots in the Dark: The Policy, Politics, and Symbolism of Gun Control* (New York: Roman and Littlefield, 2000), Wendy Cukier and Victor W. Sidel's *The Global Gun Epidemic: From Saturday Night Specials to AK-47s* (Westport, CT: Praeger Security International, 2006), John Lott's *More Guns, Less Crime: Understanding Crime and Gun Control Laws* (Chicago: University of Chicago Press, 1998), and Jan E. Dizar, Robert Muth, and Stephen Andrews's *Guns in America: A Reader* (New York: New York University Press, 1999). Gary Kleck and Don B. Kates have contributed two noteworthy studies, *The Great American Gun Debate: Essays on Firearms and Violence* (San Francisco: Pacific Research Institute for Public Policy, 1997) and *Armed: New Perspectives on Gun Control* (Amherst, NY: Prometheus Books, 2001), as have Philip J. Cook and Jens Ludwig, authors of *Guns in America: Results of a Comprehensive Survey of Gun Ownership and Use* (Washington, DC: National Institute of Justice, 1997) and *Gun Violence: The Real Costs* (New York: Oxford University Press, 2000). On children and firearms, see Ted Schwarz's *Kids and Guns: The History, the Present, the Dangers, and the Remedies* (New York: Franklin Watts, 1999) and Joseph F. Sheley and James D. Wright's *In the Line of Fire: Youth, Guns, and Violence in Urban America* (New York: Aldine de Gruyter, 1995).

Finally, works such as Charles Derber's *The Wilding of America: How Greed and Violence Are Eroding Our Nation's Character* (New York: St. Martin's Press, 1996) and Sissela Bok's *Mayhem: Violence as Public Entertainment* (Reading, MA: Perseus Books, 1998) provide critiques and exposés of the culture of violence. James Gilligan's *Violence: Reflections on a National Epidemic* (New York: Vintage, 1997) offers one doctor's viewpoint. David Griffith's *A Good War Is Hard to Find: The Art of Violence in America* (Brooklyn: Soft Skull Press, 2006) is superlative. Anthony Burgess's novel *A Clockwork Orange* (New York: Norton, 1963) still resonates, as does Stanley Kubrick's film adaptation.

Index